KU-790-330

For Alex

THIS IS A CARLTON BOOK

Design and special photography
copyright © 2001 Carlton Books Limited
Text copyright © 2001 Rose Dale
First published in 2001. This paperback
edition published in 2003 by
Carlton Books Limited
20 Mortimer Street, London W1T 3JW

A CIP catalogue record for this book is available
from the British Library
ISBN 1 84442 969 5

Printed and bound in Dubai

Editorial Manager: Venetia Penfold
Art Director: Penny Stock
Senior Art Editor: Barbara Zuñiga
Project Editor: Zia Mattocks
Editor: Sian Parkhouse
Special Photography: Catherine Gratwicke
Stylist: Hilary Robertson
Production Controller: Marianna Wolf

SMALL GARDENS, BIG IDEAS

easy gardening
& stylish decorating
for outdoor spaces

Rose Dale

CARLTON
BOOKS

CONTENTS

INTRODUCTION

A small garden is a wonderful thing. The perfect antidote to modern-day living, it can provide a tranquil green haven, hours of therapeutic pottering and more room to party. What could be better than lounging in a hammock with a glass of wine (and your mobile phone, if you must), dining under a palm tree or picking home-grown tomatoes in your own little garden?

Exploiting any outside space, whether it's a window sill, back yard or roof terrace, clearly makes good sense. As property prices soar and people cram into smaller and smaller homes, an outdoor room is an important extension to your living space. It can provide a summer kitchen, a second living room, a playroom or a fabulous venue for entertaining. Even if there's no space for an outdoor room, using blank walls and window ledges as growing space produces wonderful views and scent-filled air, dramatically changing the atmosphere of your home. Into the bargain, a beautiful garden, whatever its size, can significantly raise the value of your property. Why invest in a stylish kitchen and a smart bathroom, but look out onto a dank basement patio or a shabby flat roof? And, of course, surrounding yourself with beauty has to be a good thing.

A garden is a great place to unwind and indulge your creative urges. You can find time and space to relax – deadlines are forgotten (plants aren't in a hurry). Growing things, whether roses or rocket, is incredibly satisfying, and messing about in the dirt makes a pleasant change from painting your nails or watching bad television. Gardening is also great exercise, and much more fun than working out at the gym.

Gone are the days when gardening was just for jam-making housewives or horticultural experts. Gardening today is about using your outdoor space to the full, and having fun designing and decorating it along the way. This new style of gardening is for busy young people. Even the most committed urbanites (people who wonder how the potatoes on the vegetable counter got so muddy) can do it – and enjoy it.

Hectic lives and demanding careers mean that, for many people, tackling the garden has to be fast, fun and hassle-free. The new gardening can be quick and simple: a splash of paint and a few squares of decking might be all that's needed. If you do have time to potter, more elaborate schemes can be undertaken. Easy-growing plants can be selected to survive inhospitable conditions and inexperienced carers. Maintenance is kept to a minimum, using hard-wearing materials and modern techniques.

Just as interior design can be cheap and chic, gaining a beautiful view or creating a room outside needn't blow the budget. Inexpensive modern materials like concrete and plastic can produce great effects, and harmonize well with contemporary architecture. Recycled and reclaimed materials can look good and cost little, too. Carry ideas from interior design outside and start planning your new dining room, albeit one with a vine-draped pergola for a ceiling.

We are not made to live in an arid, built-up environment. Plants, sunlight and fresh air are good for the soul. All too often, outside space is neglected or simply not appreciated. So banish any preconceptions or worries about gardening; indulge yourself, be creative and get the most out of the little bit of the great outdoors that you are lucky enough to have. How can you resist it?

LEFT A SMALL CITY GARDEN HAS BEEN MADE INTO A BLISSFUL GREEN HAVEN, WITH AN ABUNDANCE OF FRAGRANT LILIES, LUSH FERNS AND IVIES, AND A PRETTY SEAT FOR SOAKING UP THE TRANQUIL ATMOSPHERE.

the space

Before you start building, painting, digging or planting, work out the best use and design for your outside space. You need to come up with a solution that is both right for you and practical in the type of space you have. Think about what you would enjoy doing in your garden, and consider your lifestyle and the qualities of the space itself, as all of these will affect the design. For example, if you love entertaining, don't fill your garden with flower beds leaving no space for guests; instead, a large terrace with built-in seating would be useful. Or, if you know you won't have time to mow the grass, opt for low-maintenance paving. And, if your garden is damp and shady, there's no point buying a sun lounger; but you could grow ferns and ivies, and illuminate it beautifully for night-time dining. Once you know what you want to do with your space, plan and equip it accordingly. Last but not least, decide on a style or theme for your garden to give it a coherent, harmonious feel. With a wide range of styles to choose from, you can have lots of fun creating the perfect look. The following sections will help you evaluate both your needs and your space, so you can create a useful and beautiful garden that you'll love.

PLANNING YOUR GARDEN

What outside space do you have available? Don't overlook niches by the front door, passageways, window ledges, flat roofs or blank walls. Plants can colonize almost anywhere and containers can be used to provide a mini-garden at any altitude (some plants even grow without soil). Once you've identified your potential garden, consider its qualities, scope and limitations, as these will impact on what you can do in it and the materials that you should use.

How big is your garden? Could it be a room, or even several distinct areas, each with a different theme? Or is it purely something to look at, rather than go into? Consider the location of your outdoor space. Is it at basement level and surrounded by high walls? Is it an overlooked balcony halfway up a building, or on a roof exposed to the elements? All of these locations have different possibilities and lend themselves to different uses. Do you live in a city? If so, your garden is probably warmer than those in less urban areas. 'The Gardens' (page 16) provides lots of advice and ideas for different types of small garden; use them to help you get your design right.

Consider the aspect, as this will make a big difference to what you can grow. Is it sunny or shady? Is it north- or south-facing? In the northern hemisphere, a south-facing wall receives the most sunlight during the day, and a west-facing corner gets the evening sun. Is your garden overshadowed by trees or buildings? Trees create dappled shade, whereas buildings cast solid, deeper shade.

Check out the soil (if there is any). Is it soggy and waterlogged, damp or bone dry? Is it sandy or gravelly? (This means it probably has good drainage.) Is it sticky? If so, it is probably a clay soil, which has poor drainage. Are there weeds? It's good if there are, as this proves the soil is fertile. What's growing well nearby? It's likely that it will grow well in your garden, too. It may also indicate whether the soil is acid or alkaline (if camellias are growing next door, it's probably acid). See plants, pages 141–53 to help you decide what to plant.

YOUR LIFESTYLE

Think about how you live, your needs and the time you have for gardening. Do you want (or need) your garden to be something beautiful to admire, a place to entertain, a sanctuary to escape from stress, somewhere to potter or a space to let the kids run amok? If you need time alone, make it a comfortable refuge, but if you love throwing parties, keep it accessible and fun. If you often get home late, make sure your garden is at its best at night (install good lighting and grow night-scented flowers). If you already use your garden, bear in mind what you like doing in it. Decide how much time, effort and cash you want to spend looking after your garden. Be realistic: it may be fun doing something now, but will it get boring or be forgotten later on? A lawn can look pretty, but it may be a chore to look after. Will you be away when the plants need watering? Can you afford a gardener? Consider how patient you are and how long you intend to live there. It may be worth investing in mature plants, so you don't have to gaze at bare walls while you wait for small ones to grow. If you are going to be there for a while, you might regret not planting the perfect (but slow-growing) tree.

RIGHT YOUR GARDEN SHOULD BE A SPACE DESIGNED FOR YOU. DECIDE WHAT YOU WANT TO DO OUT THERE AND THEN PLAN AND EQUIP IT SO YOU CAN DO JUST THAT. IF YOU WANT TO SPEND PRECIOUS SPARE TIME RELAXING WITH A BOOK RATHER THAN WEEDING OR MOWING THE LAWN, A PAVED GARDEN WITH EASY EVERGREEN BAMBOO AND IVY WILL PROVIDE THE PERFECT LOW-MAINTENANCE SOLUTION.

LEFT IF YOU ARE A PLANTAHOLIC, DESIGN YOUR GARDEN WITH PLENTY OF GROWING SPACE. A BORDER 3 METRES (10 FEET) WIDE IS NOT ABSURD. RESIST THE TEMPTATION TO SCALE EVERYTHING DOWN JUST BECAUSE YOU ARE WORKING IN A SMALL SPACE. IT IS FAR BETTER TO MAKE A FEW BOLD STATEMENTS THAN TO EMULATE A COUNTRY HOUSE GARDEN IN MINIATURE.

RIGHT AN UNATTRACTIVE FLAT ROOF HAS BEEN CONVERTED INTO A DELIGHTFUL OUTDOOR ROOM. A PANEL OF SANDBLASTED GLASS, LAID FLUSH WITH THE DECKING, PRESERVES LIGHT IN THE ROOM BELOW, AND SIMPLE METAL STRUTS DEFINE AN INTIMATE LIVING SPACE. HANDSOME TERRACOTTA URNS PROVIDE DECORATION AND LOOK BEST LEFT EMPTY.

USING YOUR GARDEN

Once you've decided what you want to do in your garden, design and equip the space to allow you to do it.

Entertaining

If you want to entertain outside, keep sufficient space free for the sort of entertaining you enjoy; for dancing or drinks parties, you'll need a fairly large terrace. Invest in garden furniture (unless you're going to carry indoor stuff outside) and good lighting. Built-in seating might be convenient, and paving provides a firm surface for people and furniture to stand on, particularly after rain. You might want a barbecue or outdoor oven, and storm lanterns to shelter candles outdoors. An awning or mini-marquee is a wise investment in rainy or hot climates, and blankets and a patio heater will keep guests cosy on cooler nights. You could grow fresh herbs like rosemary, basil and parsley for cooking, and cucumbers and borage flowers for garnishing punch. Pots of flowering plants provide decoration and save a last minute trip to the florist's.

Relaxing

You'll need places to laze and live life in the slow lane – a hammock under a tree, well-designed sun loungers, mats and cushions for lying on. Pads make outdoor furniture far more comfortable and blankets keep you warm when it's chilly. Make tempting places to sit and surround them with scented plants like lavender and jasmine. Position chairs or benches to catch the sun at different times of the day. Plant easy-to-grow flowers and choose low-maintenance paving and boundaries so you can concentrate on lazing about. Install a still pool to aid meditative reflection and, to really switch off, place slices of home-grown cucumbers over your eyes!

Amusing the children

Whether or not you're a parent, you'll probably have children visiting from time to time. A garden is a great place for them to play in and, with the right equipment, you can keep them out of mischief (and your hair) for hours. With children on the loose, a garden needs to be safe (and hard-wearing), but make it fun and interesting for them, too.

Leave room for children to run around, ride bikes and play ball. In a limited space, don't go overboard with climbing frames, swings and slides, but if you've got the space, a wigwam or playhouse can be their own little domain, while a resilient shrubbery could be used to make secret dens. Sandpits (sandboxes) are excellent for keeping young children entertained, providing hours of build-up and bash-down fun (make sure yours has a lid to keep rain and pets out). You needn't make a built-in version: free-standing plastic types can be emptied and put away in winter or when you have a grown-up party.

plants, page 149), and plants that look good in more than one season; perhaps a small tree with spring flowers and beautiful autumn foliage (see multi-talented plants, page 145). Plants in containers can be enjoyed in a prime position and moved out of sight when they are past their best. Use a beautiful piece of sculpture (see page 131) or a water feature (see pages 126–9) as a focal point – consider lining it up with the centre of any French doors or a window you often look out of to link the garden with the architecture of the house.

Pottering

To use your garden as a place to grow or make things, you'll need plenty of growing space and a convenient work area. Design wide flower beds (with stepping-stone paths through them so all the plants are easily accessible). A sturdy potting bench or table could be used for working on; make room underneath it to store empty pots, seed trays, sacks of compost (potting soil) and other equipment. A mini-greenhouse or cold frame lets you nurture less robust plants (and looks pretty, too). You might want a shed or larger greenhouse for pottering in bad weather, or a heated greenhouse for growing exotic plants. Stock up with well-made tools, comfortable gloves, practical plant labels and attractive containers. If you've got the right equipment and space to work, raising seeds and cuttings, and nurturing plants is lots of fun.

Buy plastic tools, flower pots and watering cans to allow little ones to join in the gardening. Leave a bare patch of soil or a few pots for them to grow easy flowers and vegetables from seed (radishes and ruby chard are very quick; sunflowers and nasturtiums are colourful).

It is crucial to keep young children away from open water, so fence off or fit strong metal grilles over any that you have in your garden. You should also take care that the plants you use are not poisonous or skin irritants, check specialist books before you purchase.

Gazing

If your garden is just for looking at, include attractive features that can easily be seen from inside the house. Perhaps a plant-smothered arch or some interesting topiary. Screen any ugly features from view and frame good vistas to heighten their impact. Illuminate the garden so you can enjoy the view at night. Select great-performing plants for spectacular borders; include some evergreens for year-round appeal, plants that flower over a long period of time (see long-flowering

Retreating

In order to escape in your garden, you'll probably want a secluded place where you can't be seen by anyone (and where you can't hear the telephone ring). If your garden is overlooked, construct an over-head framework of beams, and stretch panels of canvas between them (that can be drawn across when you want) or simply drape loose fabric over them. Trellis or folding screens can also be used to make private areas. Drown out any sound of traffic with gurgling water features and rustling grasses. Scented plants and outdoor candles have a calming effect (and some keep insects away). Make wide flower beds for thick, enshrouding planting and create small, intimate areas for sitting. Plants with dense, evergreen foliage grown along the boundaries will add to the sense of protection and enclosure, while white flowers will create a feeling of serenity.

YOUR GARDEN STYLE

Before you embark on designing and decorating your garden, decide on a style or theme. Consider the overall look you want, and make sure it will work in your outside space and fit in with your lifestyle. For example, in a dark basement, a sun-baked Mediterranean or hot desert style is probably out of the question, but the magical atmosphere of a shaded woodland might be easy to create. If you've got children, an immaculate Italianate water garden isn't a good idea, but a relaxed seaside feel (without the water) could be fun.

Go for a style that ties in with your home: with both the external architecture and the interior design. If you live in a modern concrete building, a romantic cottage garden just won't work. Linking the style of your interior and exterior decoration will make the outside space feel part of the home and both areas seem bigger. Above all, choose a look that really appeals to you and that you will have fun with. There's a huge range of different styles and themes to choose from. You may be inspired by a country or culture, a habitat, a colour or simply a material. Jungle, Japanese, minimalist, Mediterranean, traditional English, American prairie – you decide, it's your private world.

When you are selecting what elements (flooring, furniture, plants and so on) to use outdoors, keep to your chosen style so that everything ties in well together and the space is pleasantly coherent. And if there are important features in your garden that you don't want to (or can't) change, take them into account when you are deciding on a style. If you already have a terrace paved in unglazed terracotta tiles, a relaxed Mediterranean feel, using terracotta pots, painted walls and plantings of lavender and herbs, might be a good option. The smaller the area, the more important it is to link the various elements. Without an underlying style, you could end up with a hilarious jumble, rather than a calm oasis. An alpine rockery, Moroccan tiled paving, Japanese sculptures, old-fashioned English roses and New Zealand tree ferns would look ridiculous all together. At the same time, you don't need to stick slavishly to a formula,

RIGHT OPT FOR A SEASIDE THEME AND USE YOUR GARDEN TO LEND A HOLIDAY ATMOSPHERE TO YOUR HOME. AN ORDINARY SHED CAN BE TRANSFORMED INTO A BEACH HUT BY PAINTING IT A PRETTY COLOUR OR IN CANDY STRIPES. USE IT TO STORE SUN UMBRELLAS, DECK CHAIRS AND OTHER COMFORTABLE FURNITURE FOR LAZING IN THE SUN, ALONG WITH CUSHIONS IN WASHED-OUT SEA BLUES AND GREENS.

and you may prefer to hint at a certain style, rather than go for full-blown overkill. If you do want to combine elements from different styles, proceed with care, and always keep the basic idea in mind as you go along. And, of course, remember that some materials, like plain terracotta pots or pale grey concrete, are fairly neutral and will work with different looks.

Related to the question of style is the choice between a formal or informal layout. Order and control characterize a formal garden; the effect is not intended to look natural. So, for a formal look, use regular, geometric shapes for terraces, pools and flower beds, and use straight lines for paths and hedges. Free-flowing curves are out, but circles and ovals fit in (you could also add a central feature, such as a large urn or sculpture). If you prefer a more relaxed and naturalistic effect, use an informal layout where straight lines are banished and man-made constructions, such as ponds, are disguised as natural occurrences. Some styles are inherently formal, like Italianate gardens or Elizabethan knot gardens, but other styles give you the option. For example, if you choose a modern minimalist style, the formal version would be regular, ordered and static, whereas the informal variation would use irregular, flowing, organic forms.

Once you have chosen the style, let it guide you as you design, build, decorate and choose plants, furniture and accessories for your garden. You'll get the best result if each element of your garden is carefully picked, so don't just settle for the first wooden fencing you see. If your garden has an Oriental theme, a bamboo fence might look better or, if it's modern, glass bricks could look far more slick. The following pages will introduce you to a gorgeous selection from the enormous range of styles that you could adopt, and give you ideas and inspiration for creating a stylish outdoor room.

the gardens

Outdoor spaces cannot all be treated in the same way. Unlike indoor rooms, gardens have properties which often can't be controlled. The most significant of these are the climate, whether it faces north or south, whether it is shaded or in sun, the degree of privacy and the nature of the soil. Although certain features can be overcome (for example, if your garden is overlooked, you may be able to put up an overhead screen), many cannot. But the fact that the great outdoors cannot be regulated makes it all the more exciting. The qualities of your garden present a challenge, and if you work with them cleverly, you will create a wonderful garden room. The following pages provide a guide to what you can achieve in a particular type of outdoor space. If your garden is shady and sheltered, the section on basements and lightwells will help, but if you have a windy, exposed space, consult the section on roof terraces and balconies. In between these extremes are back gardens and front gardens, for which different considerations apply, and the final section will make sure you get your window containers just right. Let the fabulous variety of different garden styles inspire you as you decide what to do with your outdoor space.

BACK GARDENS & COURTYARDS

There's no need to put up with an unappealing and impractical back garden that you only venture out into when it's too nice to stay indoors. Make it a beautiful, inviting and useful space that enhances the inside of your home and lures you outside for alfresco fun.

A GORGEOUS BACKDROP

Maximize the benefits of your back garden by making sure it looks just as good from indoors as outdoors. A well-designed back garden can provide a delightful tableau and make the inside of your home really special. What could be more lovely than enchanting vistas out onto colourful flowers, cool green foliage and appealing places to sit? For greater variety, add features such as unusual pieces of sculpture, a leafy pergola or dramatically illuminated water.

Place pots of flowers, fountains or accessories where they can be seen from indoors. Grow pretty climbers around windows and doors to frame the view – scented flowers would be a bonus and could also be appreciated inside. Stand indoors and look out through the back door and any important windows (like one over the kitchen sink or near your dining table) when you are deciding how to lay out your back garden. Make sure the design works from inside (where you'll be for much of the time).

LEFT GARDEN DESIGN NEEDN'T BE COMPLICATED; A FEW WELL-CHOSEN ELEMENTS CAN CREATE AN IDYLLIC PLACE FOR A QUIET DRINK. POSITION POTS OF LAVENDER ON A SMALL PAVED AREA AND ADD A PRETTY TABLE AND CHAIRS. IF THERE ARE GAPS IN PAVING, GROW SMALL PLANTS IN THEM: CREEPING THYMES WILL RELEASE FRAGRANCE WHEN CRUSHED UNDERFOOT; DWARF BELLFLOWERS (SUCH AS *CAMPANULA PORTENSCHLAGIANA*) WILL SELF-SEED WITH MERRY ABANDON.

MAKE A SMALL BACK GARDEN SEEM BIGGER

The archetypal urban back garden is long and narrow, and is often enclosed by a high fence or wall. Beat the shoe-box impression by using the following devices:

- Make sure the whole garden can't be seen at a glance. Use screens to create areas that aren't instantly visible. This gives an air of mystery and draws people out to explore.
- Create different levels to alleviate monotony – a raised deck, raised flower beds (not just along the edges, try some jutting out across the garden), a raised pond or steps up to a terrace could work wonders.
- Instead of laying paving or a lawn parallel to the house wall, lay it at a 45-degree angle. This turns the line of vision to the diagonal so you don't just stare straight down the garden.
- A well-placed tree stops the space from looking flat and dull (see great small garden trees, page 28, and multi-talented plants, pages 145–6).
- Get together with your neighbours and find out if they will agree to remove part of the boundary fence so you can enjoy each other's gardens (you can always keep some of the fence for privacy). Replace a high fence with one built to half-height and topped by trellis.
- To disguise the limits of the space, use thick planting around the boundaries.
- Use mirrors to create the illusion of extra space. A carefully positioned mirror in an archway or surrounded by foliage can look like an opening through to another garden room (see mirrors, page 118).
- Still or moving water enlivens the garden scene, detracting from the limits of the space and focusing interest on what's contained in the garden (see water, pages 126–30).

LEFT EXOTIC EVERGREEN PALMS
AND COLOURFUL POTS, FURNITURE AND
ACCESSORIES WILL LOOK GOOD ALL YEAR
LONG, PREVENTING THE GARDEN FROM
BECOMING DRAB IN THE COOLER MONTHS.
THE COLOURS IN THE GARDEN ARE PICKED
UP IN THE DOOR HANGING, LINKING THE
INTERIOR AND EXTERIOR SPACES.

RIGHT MAKE YOUR GARDEN INVITING
SO IT BECOMES AN EXTENSION OF YOUR
LIVING SPACE. A WELL-FURNISHED OUT-
DOOR ROOM WILL BE FAR MORE APPEALING
AND FAR BETTER USED. IN THIS MODERN
GARDEN, METAL BEAMS, VERTICAL SCREENS
AND A LOW-LEVEL TABLE CREATE AN
ALLURING, INTIMATE SPACE.

YEAR-ROUND PLANTING

Unlike a roof terrace, which you may not see from indoors in winter, the back garden is in the spotlight all year long (even if you aren't actually in it). So make sure the planting looks good throughout the whole year. You don't want a blaze of colour for one month and a drab mess for the other eleven. You could grow plants from each of the following categories:

- Plants that look good in more than one season, such as those with pretty flowers in spring and colourful autumn leaf tints. See multi-talented plants, pages 145–6.
- Evergreen plants will make sure your garden doesn't look dull and bare in winter (and they are easy to look after as they don't require much pruning or autumn leaf-sweeping). See shade-tolerant evergreens, page 85, and, for sun-loving evergreens, see super spiky plants, page 35, and silver and blue plants, page 64.
- Plants that flower for ages (why grow something that flowers for just a week when an equally lovely plant flowers for a whole month?). See long-flowering plants, page 149.

- Plants with handsome foliage. Even if they are not evergreen, leaves last a lot longer than flowers, so use plenty of plants with beautiful leaves. See plants with great green leaves and golden plants, page 147; purple-leaved plants, pages 143–4; groovy grasses, page 152; and silver and blue plants, page 64.
- Plants that are in their prime at different times of year. Many plants look their best in late spring and early summer. Make sure you grow flowers for other seasons, too (particularly late summer when you're most likely to be outside to enjoy them).
- Where space is at a premium, grow climbers. Choose different types for foliage and year-round flowers (see climbers for shady gardens, page 86, and easy climbers, page 142).

CREATING AN ENTICING SPACE

Make outdoors feel more accessible by blurring the boundaries between inside and out. If your garden appears to be unrelated to the inside space, you will continue to view it as a separate and distinct area, and probably won't use it as often as you would if you made it work with the interior. Make sure the doors leading into the garden are easy to open (and the key to them is kept to hand). Consider installing floor-to-ceiling doors so you can claim the outside as part of your living space on balmy days. Have the door track recessed so furniture can easily be pushed outdoors whenever you want. Why use a rickety garden chair when you could laze on a comfortable sofa stolen from inside?

Create wide and generous flights of steps leading into the garden. Steep, narrow steps running into the main garden make it appear cut-off and uninviting (and are perilous when you're carrying a

tray of drinks). Although replacing a flight of steps is a major investment, it will greatly improve the outlook from indoors and will also increase the amount you use the garden. Go for it.

Link the decor of the indoor and outdoor spaces. Use the same colours and materials inside and out: for example, an uninterrupted row of identical planters could extend outside, or you could grow more delicate varieties of your outdoor plants indoors.

SOMEWHERE TO HANG OUT

A back garden is prime space for outdoor living, particularly when it leads off the kitchen, as you can easily eat and entertain out there in fine weather. Decide where you enjoy sitting and lazing, and create terraces and arbours to suit your needs. Before you automatically site a terrace next to the house, ask yourself whether it's really the best place for it. If the far end of the garden gets the afternoon and evening sun, that may be the ideal spot for a dining table and chairs. Make a choice of places to sit to suit different moods and times of day. A tiny table in the part of the garden that gets the early morning sun is perfect for breakfast. Or you may want a peaceful, shaded place to read, or a secluded hot spot for sunbathing. If your garden is overlooked, use overhead structures (see pages 119–20) to create intimate places to relax in. A few wires supporting a climber may be enough to obscure the view from above and give a feeling of privacy.

Grow a mix of fragrant plants that will be at their best when you're outside on warm summer and autumn days (see summer scented plants, page 42). Plant them where they'll be appreciated: close to pathways, doors and sitting areas.

LOW-MAINTENANCE 'LAWNS'

You don't have to keep the lawn just because it's already there. Most city gardens work better without one because they are too shady and well-used for the grass to thrive. To look good, a lawn needs so much mind-numbing maintenance – mowing, feeding, watering, weeding, spiking – that there might be no time left over to lie on it and enjoy it. Can you really be bothered to look after it? Paving won't die off in patches and doesn't get too muddy to use. Need I say more?

If you really want to have a pool of green in a shady spot, why not use vigorous ground-cover plants that will look after themselves. Try thickly planted bugle (*Ajuga*), periwinkle (*Vinca*) or mind-your-own-business (*Soleirolia soleirolii*)? Failing that, opt for hassle-free (and funky) plastic grass. If you must have a traditional lawn, use a slow-growing variety of grass and keep the lawn shape simple and free of island flower beds so at least it's easy to mow.

Large areas of one type of flooring can look dull, so break them up by using two different types of material: in sunny gardens, you could team decking with cobblestones, or try a mixture of concrete and glass for a modern look. Natural stone and brick is a traditional combination that works well with period buildings.

A back garden is often seen from above, so think about how it will appear from the upper floors of your home. Attractive patterns in paving can look good from upstairs rooms even if they aren't immediately obvious at ground level.

FAR LEFT MIXED HARD SURFACES CAN ENLIVEN A SMALL PAVED GARDEN – EXPERIMENT TO FIND MATERIALS THAT BLEND WELL TOGETHER AND THAT ALSO FIT IN WITH THE ARCHITECTURAL STYLE OF YOUR HOME. YOU COULD LAY DIFFERENT MATERIALS IN INTERESTING PATTERNS THAT WILL LOOK GOOD WHEN SEEN FROM THE UPPER WINDOWS OF YOUR HOME, ADDING ANOTHER DIMENSION TO THE DESIGN.

LEFT IF YOU'VE GOT THE SPACE, PERMANENT GARDEN FURNITURE MAKES FOR EASY OUTDOOR LIVING – YOU CAN JUST CARRY TRAYS OF DRINKS AND PLATES OF FOOD OUTSIDE. DECORATE AN OUTDOOR TABLE WITH STYLISH PLACE MATS AND BOLD FOLIAGE HARVESTED FROM THE GARDEN (ONE OR TWO BIG BRANCHES OR ARCHITECTURAL LEAVES WOULD MAKE A REFRESHING CHANGE).

You may not want to have furniture cluttering up a small garden space all year round. Instead, buy light indoor tables and chairs that you can easily carry outside whenever you need them, or get folding furniture that can be stashed away in the shed when you aren't using it. If you've got room, a garden shed is the best storage solution and it can be decorated so that it looks charming. Other options include built-in wooden cupboards, stacks of large plastic boxes or box seating.

I DON'T CARE WHAT THE WEATHERMAN SAYS

An awning or marquee is a great way to extend your entertaining space, no matter what the weather. Simply put up a tarpaulin, attaching one edge by hooks to the side of the house and tying the other to trees or posts, or get a roll-up one installed on the side of the house. More elaborate tent constructions with side walls could be commissioned if your budget permits. A broad-striped canvas would suit a traditional garden, while shiny silver fabric might look good in an modern space. For evening, use a midnight-blue awning and string rows of fairy lights underneath for a mock starry sky.

Lighting and garden heaters can also be employed to extend the use of your space, especially if you're usually only at home in the evening (see lighting, pages 124–5, and accessories & tools, pages 132–4). A barbecue or outdoor oven might be a worthwhile investment. If you don't have anywhere to store it, make sure you get an attractive version so the stark beauty of your winter garden isn't spoilt.

COURTYARDS

Courtyards are special places. Enclosed by walls or buildings, they are sheltered and protected, and have their own unique ambience. If your outside space has these characteristics, don't yearn for spectacular views of rolling countryside (or city roof tops). Revel in the sense of enclosure and create your own Turkish seraglio or Moorish palace, complete with rugs, candles and a petal-strewn pool, or design an Elizabethan-style fortress (you could even put mock battlements along the walls).

City courtyards are particularly well shielded from the elements. Frosts are less likely (especially if the courtyard is surrounded by heated buildings) and the temperature will certainly never plummet as low as it does in exposed country gardens. Wind and draughts may also be excluded. Exploit this favourable microclimate and indulge in unusual and exotic tender plants, including some scented plants whose fragrance will linger in the still air (see special plants for sheltered gardens, page 92).

TROPICAL

Chase away the cold-weather blues by going all-out exotic. Palms, bananas and yuccas will remind you of tropical climes (and far-flung holiday destinations). Add brightly coloured flowers and furnishings – who needs the Caribbean? Just get a hot-pink parasol to keep the rain off, sit back and pretend you're on vacation. Resist the urge to go for tasteful colour harmony; the more vibrant the hues, the better. Hunt for sizzlingly hot-coloured flowers, fuchsia and scarlet cushions, bright yellow candles, colourful glazed pots and tropical-style plants. Some wonderfully exotic-looking plants are suprisingly tough and hardy. Position them in a sheltered spot (out of cold wind, which is particularly damaging), don't overwater them and they should withstand low temperatures and gloomy days. Or grow them indoors and carry them outside for a summer break on the patio. (See jungle plants, pages 142–3, and super spiky plants, page 35.)

FIERY FLOWERS

Get totally tropical with sizzling orange, red and yellow flowers. Add deep purple or bronze foliage to make the colours seem even more vivid.

- Montbretia (*Crocosmia*): Sword-like foliage and arching spikes of fiery summer flowers that are great for cutting. 'Lucifer' has devilish scarlet flowers, 'Jackanapes' has red and orange, 'Golden Fleece' has bright yellow. It dies down to ground level in winter.
- Lilies (*Lilium*): Look for blazing colours like 'Citronella' (spotty bright yellow), 'Enchantment' (rich orange) and 'Fire King' (purple-spotted vivid red).

- Red-hot pokers (*Kniphofia*): Dramatic spikes of bright flowers. Look for 'Prince Igor' (scarlet) and 'Royal Standard' (yellow at the bottom, orange at the top).
- Maltese Cross (*Lychnis chalcedonica*): Clusters of small scarlet flowers. Deadhead regularly to keep the flowers coming from late June to August. It needs support and will self-seed freely if you don't cut the faded flowers off.

All these plants can be planted outside and should come up year after year. Fill any gaps with colourful easy annuals like nasturtiums and marigolds.

REVAMP YOUR PAVING

Don't resign yourself to putting up with ugly paving because it's too expensive or too much work to dig up and replace. Even really dreary, uninteresting slabs can be transformed to look fantastic by the clever use of masonry paint. A single, solid colour might look just the thing in a minimal or starkly modern space, but blending two similar, natural tones gives a textural, organic look that may suit your garden better. If you have square slabs, you could get creative and paint a geometric pattern or chequerboard effect. Either use toning shades for a subtle look (try echoing the natural greens of your plants) or use dramatically contrasting colours for a bold statement.

1 Here, the garden owners took two different-coloured terracotta pots into a specialist paint shop and had paint shades mixed up to match.

2 They then painted the existing multicoloured crazy paving slabs in the darkest shade of paint, leaving the mortar in between the slabs its original colour so that the pattern was retained.

3 The slabs were then given a 'weathered' appearance with patchy application of the lighter terracotta colour over the top of the original coat.

4 In areas of heavy wear, you can apply several coats of paint for a lasting effect. Keep some paint so you can touch up scuffed slabs when necessary.

LEFT TEXTILES ARE A GREAT WAY TO ADD INSTANT COLOUR TO AN OUTDOOR SPACE AND A FOLDAWAY FLORAL MATTRESS CAN PROVIDE A PERFECT PLACE FOR LOUNGING. WHEN THE WEATHER LOOKS PROMISING, TAKE THE MATTRESS OUT ONTO THE TERRACE FOR TOTAL COMFORT OUTDOORS – A FEW CUSHIONS WILL MAKE IT REALLY SUMPTUOUS. YOU COULD EVEN SPEND THE NIGHT UNDER THE STARS.

ABOVE RIGHT COBALT-BLUE CERAMIC STOOLS LOOK ATTRACTIVE AND CAN BE MOVED ABOUT FOR DIFFERENT EFFECTS.

THEY DOUBLE UP AS GARDEN ROOM DIVIDERS, AS WELL AS MAKING PERFECT TABLES AND PLANT STANDS.

RIGHT CRUSHED GLASS COMES IN A KALEIDOSCOPE OF COLOURS; USE IT IN THE TOP OF PLANT POTS FOR A SPLASH OF INSTANT COLOUR AND TO OFFSET PLAIN GREEN FOLIAGE. THE GLASS CHIPS ALSO PREVENT EVAPORATION AND HELP KEEP THE COMPOST (POTTING SOIL) DAMP. A TERRACOTTA PLANT LABEL THAT MATCHES THE POT LOOKS FAR BETTER THAN A WHITE PLASTIC ONE.

GREAT SMALL GARDEN TREES

- Aconite-leafed maple (*Acer japonicum* 'Aconitifolium'): This has extremely pretty, lacy leaves that are fresh green when they appear in spring and turn a rich red in the autumn. It produces many clusters of reddish flowers in spring.

- Japanese maples (*Acer palmatum*): This wonderful group of trees have beautiful foliage that acquires spectacular autumn leaf tints. Many grow very slowly, so they are perfect in tiny spaces and will also do well in a pot. The type called 'Garnet' has filigree red-purple leaves, 'Burgundy Lace' has palmate, dark purple leaves, while 'Linearilobum' has spiky, bright green leaves that turn orange and yellow in autumn.

- Silver birch (*Betula utilis* var. *jacquemontii*): This has a light, airy structure, beautiful white bark and dainty leaves that turn yellow in autumn. You can buy trees with single trunks or, for a change, look for multi-stemmed specimens.

- Pagoda dogwood (*Cornus alternifolia* 'Argentea'): This grows in horizontal layers to produce a striking, tiered effect and has lovely variegated leaves that are green with white margins. It bears flat clusters of tiny white flowers in summer, followed by blue-black fruit.

- Weeping silver pear (*Pyrus salicifolia* 'Pendula'): A delightful small deciduous tree with silvery leaves on branches that droop down to the ground. It has white flowers in spring.

- Star magnolia (*Magnolia stellata*): A small, deciduous magnolia that can be grown in a container. It has star-like flowers (in pink or white) in early spring.

- Kilmarnock willow (*Salix caprea* 'Kilmarnock'): A diminutive weeping willow, that bears fluffy silver catkins on its bare twigs in late winter.

- Snow gum (*Eucalyptus pauciflora* subsp. *niphophila*): This has smooth, ghostly white twigs and branches, and slim, greyish evergreen leaves.

RIGHT MAKE THE MOST OF YOUR PLANTS BY CLEVERLY DESIGNING THE SURROUNDINGS TO ACCENTUATE THEIR BEST FEATURES. THE DARK-PAINTED FENCE BEHIND THE SILVER BIRCH TREES (*BETULA*) HIGHLIGHTS THEIR SILVERY BARK AND THE RIGID WHITE PANELS DISPLAY THEIR DELICATE SHADOW PATTERNS BEAUTIFULLY.

MODERN

Modern buildings and interiors may be best complemented by a modern garden. Traditional gardens, full of old-fashioned materials in standard, well-known or derivative designs can sit uncomfortably as part of a modern home. Instead, use innovative designs and contemporary building materials such as concrete, steel and glass, both to echo the surrounding environment and to put your garden at the cutting edge.

Utilitarian elements can be beautiful if employed with sensitivity; lead or copper piping, railway sleepers, concrete blocks and plastic pots all have a pleasing functionality and can appear even more attractive when placed in a new context. You could flout convention, perhaps using dustbins as planters, or growing edible plants (such as cabbages or carrots – both have marvellous foliage) as decorative elements alongside plants that are long-established as aesthetically acceptable. Or you could reinvent traditional designs with a novel, high-tech or industrial slant. A wooden or wrought-iron pergola mutates into an industrial superstructure when constructed out of iron girders; box hedges could be trimmed to look like a dinosaur's spiny back and paths could be paved in rubber tiles instead of terracotta or brick.

Just about any plant can be used in a modern garden – it's the way they are used that makes the difference. Think about how plants will look together and avoid traditional or clichéd plant combinations. And consider how plants are to be laid out: planting in geometric blocks, undulating waves or rigid lines might create a new or up-to-date effect.

ABOVE LEFT MASSIVE IRON GIRDERS WITH A RUSTED FINISH CREATE A WONDERFULLY MODERN OVERHEAD STRUCTURE THAT CLEARLY DEFINES A ROOM-LIKE SPACE WITH ITS STRONG ARCHITECTURAL LINES – PERFECT FOR OUTDOOR LIVING.
LEFT FLUID AND INTRICATE LEAF SHAPES PROVIDED BY BULLRUSHES AND FERNS COUNTERBALANCE THE SHARP, CLEAN GEOMETRY OF THE METAL BEAMS.
RIGHT A PRECISELY GEOMETRIC TABLE FITS IN BEAUTIFULLY, ECHOING THE CLEAN, STRAIGHT LINES OF THE SUPERSTRUCTURE, WHEREAS CURVACEOUS ACCESSORIES BEGIN TO FALL SWAY TO THE INFLUENCE OF ORGANIC PLANT FORMS.

Hard-wearing modern materials can be used for flooring that needs little attention. Try railway sleepers, decking, gravel or crushed stone (laid over a geo-textile membrane, which is porous but suppresses weeds). Galvanized steel is weatherproof and virtually maintenance-free. Use it for making plant containers or ultra-modern walls that reflect the light. Plastic is another good low-maintenance material. Look for furniture, plant pots and boxes; you could even get some plastic grass (astroturf) for the ultimate low-maintenance lawn. Finally, choose modern varieties and hybrids of traditional plants, which will often be easier to grow, more resistant to disease and flower for longer than their old-fashioned parents.

GET THE LOOK

- **Flooring**: High tech – sand-blasted or crushed glass, rubber, polished or dyed concrete; industrial – textured in-situ concrete, railway sleepers, rusted steel (corten).
- **Walls and screens**: Concrete blocks, in-situ concrete, metal panels, glass bricks, wire mesh, steel grilles, mirrors.
- **Furniture**: Plastic loungers, concrete stools, rubber mattresses, glass tables, anything Perspex.
- **Water**: Basins of pale concrete or black rubber, polished stone or glass with water flowing over it. For a bizarre look, recycle waste to construct a postmodern fountain using parts of old machines, from engines to typewriters.
- **Lighting**: Recessed metallic lights, fibre-optic lighting, neon lights and light projectors.

LEFT AN ULTRA-MODERN GARDEN IS ENHANCED BY A SCREEN THAT HAS MORE IN COMMON WITH A SUBMARINE THAN A TRADITIONAL GARDEN WALL. THE REFLECTIVE METAL SURFACE BRIGHTENS THE SHADY PART OF THE GARDEN AND THE CIRCULAR PORTHOLE ALLOWS ENTICING GLIMPSES OF THE NEXT GARDEN ROOM. SCREENING PART OF THE GARDEN FROM VIEW CREATES MYSTERY AND LURES PEOPLE OUT TO EXPLORE THE AREA BEYOND.

MODULAR PLASTIC CUBES ARE INFINITELY VERSATILE: STACKED UP TOGETHER THEY FORM SHELVING FOR DISPLAYING ACCESSORIES AND PLANTS. UNSTACK THEM AND REARRANGE THEM FOR TABLES AND SEATS WHEN YOUR FRIENDS DROP BY. PLACE THEM OPEN-END-DOWN AND PUT CONTAINERIZED PLANTS INSIDE THEM TO DISGUISE UNATTRACTIVE POTS (SMALLER PLANTS CAN BE RAISED UP ON BRICKS PLACED ON THE GROUND).

LEFT THE 'PORTHOLE' IN THE METAL GARDEN DIVIDER IS FITTED WITH SLIDING GLASS DOORS THAT CAN BE LOCKED FOR EXTRA SECURITY OR TO CONTAIN CHILDREN WHERE THEY CAN BE SEEN FROM INDOORS. THE RIVETS HOLDING THE METAL PANELS IN PLACE CONSTITUTE DECORATION AND ENHANCE THE INDUSTRIAL FEEL.

ABOVE HEAVY-DUTY RAILWAY SLEEPERS ARE USED AS FLOORING INSTEAD OF TRADITIONAL GARDEN DECKING. THESE, TOO, ADD TO THE INDUSTRIAL FEEL. THEY ARE INEXPENSIVE AND GREAT FOR AREAS WHICH GET A LOT OF WEAR AND TEAR AS THEY'LL LAST WELL. BUT THEY MAY SPLINTER AND LEECH TAR, SO THEY ARE NO GOOD FOR LOUNGING OR WALKING ON WITH BARE FEET, OR FOR CRAWLING BABIES.

ABOVE RIGHT GROW SOME SPIKY PLANTS FOR A DYNAMIC ELEMENT TO YOUR GARDEN. NEW ZEALAND FLAX (*PHORMIUM TENAX*) HAS LONG POINTED EVERGREEN LEAVES. SOME TYPES HAVE FOLIAGE WHICH GRACEFULLY ARCHES; SOME HAVE STIFFLY UPRIGHT LEAVES. FOR ADDED DRAMA, LOOK FOR EYE-CATCHINGLY STRIPED VARIETIES LIKE *PHORMIUM* 'SUNDOWNER' (SHOWN). THE TALL SPIKES OF OUTLANDISH FLOWERS THAT APPEAR WHEN THE PLANT IS HAPPY IN ITS POSITION ARE A SUMMER BONUS.

RIGHT SEA HOLLY (*ERYNGIUM*) HAS EXQUISITE SPIKY FLOWER HEADS. DIFFERENT VARIETIES HAVE FLOWERS THAT RANGE FROM PURPLE-TINGED GREEN TO SILVERY GREY TO ELECTRIC BLUE, AND MANY HAVE A METALLIC SHEEN.

SUPER SPIKY PLANTS

Spiky plants grab attention, giving the garden energy and excitement.

- Yuccas, Spanish dagger (*Yucca gloriosa*): This has dramatic rosettes of rigid, sharp-pointed green leaves. If grown in a hot spot, it will flower in most years. There is a yellow-striped variety, too. Adam's needle (*Yucca filamentosa*) has lance-like leaves that are fringed with tangled cottony threads. Grow all yuccas in full sun and avoid soggy soil.

- Cabbage palm (*Cordyline australis*): A palm-like tree that looks a bit like a yucca with a trunk (it can grow up to 10 m (30 ft) tall in its native New Zealand, but don't worry, it won't happen overnight) and forms an exuberant clump of pointy leaves. It comes in plain green, or look for more exotic versions like 'Albertii' (green, cream, red and pink striped leaves) and 'Torbay Dazzler' (bold green and cream stripes). Grow it somewhere sheltered; it's not desperately hardy but it should survive fine in most city gardens.

- Century plant (*Agave americana*): This is a 'wow' plant. Its leaves are rigid and thickly fleshy with sharp spines at the end and prickly margins. It comes in plain green or with yellow or white stripes. The striped types are less hardy than the plain green and need to be taken indoors in winter. Grow in full sun and well-drained soil.

- *Astelia chathamica* 'Silver Spear': Gorgeous silvery spikes. Grow in sun or part shade somewhere protected.

- New Zealand flax (*Phormium tenax*): Upright, sword-like leaves. Apart from plain green or purple there are multicoloured varieties. Try 'Sundowner' with tropical bronze- and pink-striped leaves (above left), 'Dazzler' with purple, pink, red and orange striped leaves or 'Variegatum' with green and creamy yellow striped leaves.

- Sea holly (*Eryngium*): Patterned green and white leaves emerge in spring followed by thistle-like spiky flower heads in summer. These herbaceous plants die back in winter, although their spiky skeletons often persist throughout the winter.

JAPANESE TEA GARDEN

A backdrop of mossy green sets the scene for this garden. Grow mind-your-own-business (*Soleirolia soleirolii*) as a quick moss-substitute to cover bare soil and creep over paving. For terraces and paths, grey gravel would work well, or use randomly spaced stepping stones and asymmetric paved areas in rough-hewn stone. Add rocks and smooth cobblestones for decoration.

To create a calm and contemplative effect, add swathes of cool greenery. Rhododendrons, bamboos and dwarf pines will provide an evergreen background against which other elements can be displayed. For cool shade and exquisite blossom, grow a Japanese flowering cherry tree. Train Japanese quince (*Chaenomeles*) against walls and fences. They flower on elegantly bare branches in winter and spring. Other key plants are azaleas, ferns, Japanese maples, flowering cherries and camellias.

In a Japanese garden, water can either be still or mobile. A waterfall, a bamboo spout or a motionless pool would fit in well (see water, pages 126–9). Provide further decoration with a stone spirit house, a recumbent Buddha or a piece of beautifully weathered driftwood. Fencing, trellis or furniture made of whole bamboo would look right. Split bamboo matting could be used to disguise existing walls and fences. True enthusiasts of the Japanese style could try clipping pines and box to make cloud-shaped topiary and bonsai.

TRANSFORM A SHED

Make your garden shed into a Japanese tea house.

1. Use reclaimed green-glazed tiles (from 1930s suburban houses) to decorate a pagoda-style roof. Nail them securely to a wooden frame which curves up at the sides.

2. Nail panels of large and small-squared trellis to the shed as decoration or even replace sections of the shed's walls with trellis for a more airy structure. Line the interior of the shed with sheets of plasterboard and paint them in Eastern designs.

3. Lay bamboo or rush matting on the floor to protect silk cushions and floor coverings. Hang up printed silk drapes and a bamboo wind chime for a finishing touch.

LEFT MOSS TRADITIONALLY COVERS THE FLOOR IN JAPANESE GARDENS (UNLIKE ZEN GARDENS, IN WHICH RAKED GRAVEL OR SAND ARE USED), BUT IT CAN BE DIFFICULT TO ESTABLISH. MIND-YOUR-OWN-BUSINESS (*SOLEIROLIA SOLEIROLII*) IS AN EASY SUBSTITUTE. ITS MAT OF TINY GREEN LEAVES CREEP OVER SOIL AND PAVING ALIKE. IT DOESN'T WEAR WELL, SO DON'T USE IT FOR PATHS OR OTHER AREAS OF HEAVY TRAFFIC.

ABOVE HORSETAIL RUSHES (*EQUISETUM*) ARE ANCIENT PLANTS THAT WERE AROUND WITH THE DINOSAURS. THEY GROW HAPPILY IN WATER AND SOME VARIETIES CAN BE GROWN IN A VASE INDOORS. THE BANDED, LEAFLESS STEMS ECHO BAMBOO IN MINIATURE AND TIE IN BEAUTIFULLY WITH A JAPANESE THEME.

MAKE YOUR GARDEN BIGGER

Back gardens that are long and narrow can be claustrophobic. Gain a greater sense of space by taking down a section of fence so you and your neighbour can enjoy each other's gardens. Here, part of the brick wall has been removed and the naturalistic pond extends into the next-door garden for double the watery paradise. The delightful view through to the diminutive bridge and well-disguised boundary fence is framed by handsome brick pillars.

DRESSING UP YOUR GARDEN

Inside the home, furniture, mirrors, pictures and ornaments are used to furnish and dress the space – and the same principles can be applied outdoors. You wouldn't leave a room empty once you'd painted the walls, so why leave a garden empty once you've put the plants in? Although simpler furniture and decoration often looks better outside, it is still essential.

When dressing up your outdoor room, you could create a real sense of occasion by erecting a mini-marquee. A larger one can be used for shelter from the sun or for retreating from the rain in unpredictable climates, while a smaller one can provide a festive backdrop or an intimate arbour. Furniture makes the space more people-friendly and enticing. Utilitarian accessories, such as inexpensive china, wirework vessels, and washable cottons and linens can be left outside in warm seasons when the garden is being used regularly; the occasional shower of rain won't do them any harm.

GROWING TOMATOES

First buy your seeds (there are different varieties for growing in a greenhouse or outdoors). Cordon varieties need training; bush varieties don't. In spring, sow two seeds per 7.5-cm (3-in) pot, following the instructions. Place them indoors on a bright window sill and keep them moist. A few weeks later, remove the weaker seedling. Plant them out when the first cluster of flower buds is visible. (Tomatoes need plenty of space, so grow them in the ground, in growing bags or in a pot no small than 23 cm (9 in). Water and feed them regularly with tomato fertilizer.

LEFT A COLOURFUL TENT, AN OLD TABLE AND WOVEN CHAIRS CREATE AN APPEALING SPOT FOR A LAID-BACK OUTDOOR MEAL. WITHOUT THEM, THE SPACE WOULD BE FAR LESS INVITING.

ABOVE RIGHT WORN ANTIQUE AND WELL-USED ACCESSORIES LOOK GREAT IN A GARDEN. THEIR LIVED-IN APPEARANCE GIVES A RELAXED FEEL AND SITS WELL IN THE OUTDOOR SCENE. A WIREWORK BOWL CAN BE LEFT OUTDOORS FOR HARVESTING HOME-GROWN TOMATOS AND FRUITS.

RIGHT IF YOU DON'T WANT TO PUNCTURE YOUR BOWLING-GREEN LAWN WITH TENT STAKES, USE A MINI-MARQUEE WITHOUT A FRAME THAT CAN SIMPLY BE SUSPENDED FROM A CONVENIENT BRANCH, AND WEIGH ITS SIDES DOWN USING LARGE STONES TUCKED INTO THE LOOPS OF ROPE.

SUMMER SCENTED PLANTS

When you position a scented plant, think about how far its fragrance will carry. In contrast, aromatic plants need to have their leaves pressed to release their full fragrance. Grow them where they will be brushed against or where they will be crushed underfoot.

- Night-scented stocks (*Matthiola longipetala* subsp. *bicornis*): These have unremarkable lilac flowers, but their scent is truly voluptuous on summer evenings. They are annuals and easy to grow from seed. Sow a few in a discreet pot before the end of spring, place it in sun or shade and keep the soil moist. When the flowers start to bloom, move the pot to a position where you can enjoy their scent.
- Lavender (*Lavandula*): These silvery-coloured bushes have highly aromatic foliage and pretty spikes of long-lasting flowers. Grow late-flowering *Lavandula* x *intermedia* 'Grappenhall' for flowers in late summer and early autumn.
- Chocolate plant (*Cosmos atrosanguineus*): This has velvety dark red flowers with a surprising (and delicious) chocolate fragrance if you get close. It likes the sun and should be taken indoors in winter (grow it in a pot so you can move it into a cool room or greenhouse). Deadhead regularly to prolong flowering from early summer to early autumn.

Other summer fragrant plants to sniff out include honeysuckle (useful in cool, shady gardens), lilies, evening primrose, mock orange (get *Philadelphus microphyllus* for a small space), common jasmine, sweet peas, tobacco plants, star jasmine and fragrant late-flowering roses (try apricot 'Evelyn' or pink 'Gertrude Jekyll').

Deliciously aromatic plants include cotton lavender, myrtle, catmint (catnip), rosemary, scented-leaf pelargoniums (these should be moved indoors during the winter months), *Artemisia* 'Powis Castle', sweet bay and thyme.

RIGHT IMMACULATE PINK LILIES AND PURE WHITE PELARGONIUMS CONTRAST WITH AN OLD PEELING WALL AND THE ANCIENT IVY, PREVENTING THE SPACE FROM HAVING AN AIR OF NEGLECT. IN THIS HIGH-WALLED GARDEN, THE LUSCIOUS FRAGRANCE OF THE LILIES WILL LINGER IN THE STILL AIR.

ROMANTIC

Delicate structures, soft colours, gentle shapes and pretty accessories unite to create a romantic atmosphere. Avoid all that is harsh or jarring; think soothing, not shocking. For instant height, drape swags of rope between tall upright posts along a boundary or flower bed and use them to support a mix of pretty climbers. Plant blowsy flowers in delicate pastels for a soft effect and add dark velvety reds and purples for depth (see purple-leaved plants, pages 143–4. Create a sense of luxurious abundance by cramming ornate terracotta pots and stone or cast-iron urns with summer bedding plants in harmonizing colours.

Pretty up plain chairs and benches with lacy cushions and floral fabrics or use rich velvets for an extravagant touch. For a gentle glow at night, dot candles and tea lights around the garden. Collect cut flowers in a wooden trug basket or use one for storing packets of seeds. Grow a row of lavender along the terrace to make a scented, flowering hedge and use arches to divide the garden and provide enchanting vistas. In darker gardens, lighten up the atmosphere by painting the walls or fences in pastel pinks or soft apricots. An arbour is the ultimate venue for romance, so make one in a secluded corner and surround it with fragrant plants (see summer scented plants, page 42).

Key plants to use are roses (see easy roses, page 46), clematis (try blue 'Perle d'Azur', pink or white *C. montana* or dark red 'Rouge Cardinal'), lady's mantle (*Alchemilla mollis*), lavender, honeysuckle, hardy geraniums, hydrangeas, catmint (catnip) and wisteria.

ABOVE LEFT FILIGREE WIREWORK, WITH ITS ORNATE DELICACY, HITS JUST THE RIGHT NOTE FOR A ROMANTIC GARDEN. A WIREWORK JARDINIÈRE IS PERFECT FOR DISPLAYING HERBS AND FLOWERS GROWING IN ATTRACTIVE WEATHERED TERRACOTTA POTS.

ABOVE RIGHT A FLIGHT OF STEPS IS TRANSFORMED WITH PALE BLUE PAINT. THE BARLEY TWIST RAILINGS AND FREE-FLOATING STAIR TREADS MAKE SURE THE STRUCTURE DOESN'T LOOK CUMBERSOME. POTS OF PINK PELARGONIUMS COMPLETE THE PRETTY EFFECT.

EASY ROSES

You can find a rose for just about any corner (as long as it's not too shady). Choose between ground-cover roses, patio roses (for containers or limited spaces), shrub roses and climbing roses. Or look for rose bushes trained into a lollipop shape (standards).

- Iceberg: A beautiful resilient white rose that flowers for weeks on end, often into December! Unfortunately, it's only faintly scented. There is a climbing version, too.

- Hedgehog rose (*Rosa rugosa*): This flowers continuously from summer to autumn. It's very prickly and makes a good hedge. To get sumptuous red hips, don't deadhead them. 'Roseraie de l'Haÿ' has sybaritic fragrant purple flowers; 'Alba' is pure white.

- 'Flower Carpet White': A wonderfully disease-resistant ground-cover rose (roses aren't usually), with showy clusters of white flowers through summer and autumn. It does well in a pot but isn't fragrant. 'Flower Carpet Pink' has shocking pink flowers.

- 'Kent': Small white ground-cover rose. It flowers continuously from summer to autumn but it isn't scented.

- 'Suffolk': A small ground-cover rose with scarlet flowers all summer, then orange-red hips. Pruning not necessary.

- Patio roses: Easy long-flowering varieties include 'Baby Love' (yellow), 'Queen Mother' (clear pink), 'The Fairy' (pale pink) and 'Sweet Dream' (peachy).

- English roses: Look for these new roses bred by David Austin in England; they have the fabulous scents and looks of the old-fashioned roses, but are longer-flowering and more resistant to disease.

- Climbing roses: Good varieties include 'Golden Showers' (yellow, happy on a north-facing wall) and 'Sympathie' (deep red flowers).

DEADHEADING YOUR PLANTS

Deadheading is simply removing the faded flowers on a plant. Many plants will stop flowering (or not flower so prolifically) if they aren't deadheaded because they begin to develop seeds and then their urge to flower is lost. To deadhead, just snip (or pinch) off the flower and its stalk, taking care not to cut off any new flower buds. Repeat regularly throughout the flowering season.

MODERN MINIMAL

A modern minimal garden can provide a calm and reflective place for relaxation, and relief from hectic schedules. Clear away all the clutter and use a clean sweep of uncomplicated paving over the floor, such as smooth in-situ concrete, sand-blasted glass or monochrome square tiles laid in straight lines. Paint busy multicoloured surfaces a uniform colour; use grey or cream in a serene space, or perhaps orange or fuchsia in a vibrant one.

Keep plant types to a minimum; too many different plant forms will spoil the effect. Use groups of the same plant in rows, waves or blocks, and single specimens of striking plants as a feature. You could grow a strip of spiky iris (*Iris pallida* and its variegated counterpart have sculptural and long-lasting leaves) for a static effect or a clump of swaying grasses for movement (see groovy grasses, page 152). Avoid formless and multicoloured planting. Weird and modern-looking plants include black lilyturf (*Ophiopogon planiscapus* 'Nigrescens'), wire-netting bush (*Corokia cotoneaster*),

lancewood (*Pseudopanax*), ornamental onions (*Allium cristophii* and *A. schubertii*) and black-stemmed bamboo (*Phyllostachys nigra*). For a softer look, try bronze fennel or feather grass.

Elemental modern sculpture or art is appropriate. A recessed pool brimming with water would blend seamlessly. Use one type of furniture and avoid the rustic or ornate; simple designs in smooth steel, tough nylon or polished wood bring understated refinement. Use containers in the same material as the flooring or furniture: galvanized steel, zinc or pale concrete are good choices.

LEFT AND ABOVE LEFT A SHEET OF SHEER WATER FLOWING OVER A GLASS AND METAL PANEL MAKES A SLEEK FEATURE THAT BRINGS DYNAMISM TO A STATIC AND FORMAL LAYOUT. THE LOW WALL IS TOPPED WITH CUSHION PADS FOR SEATING WHEN THE GARDEN IS USED FOR ENTERTAINING.

ABOVE KEEP A SPACE UNCLUTTERED WITH VIRTUALLY INVISIBLE SEATING. A BENCH CAN BE CONSTRUCTED BY BOLTING BRACKETS ONTO ADJACENT HEAVY, FLAT-SIDED PLANTERS AND THEN POSITIONING WOODEN PLANKS ACROSS THE BRACKETS BETWEEN THE TWO PLANTERS.

MOROCCAN COURTYARD

Conjure up the sunbaked days and sultry nights of Arabian North
Africa. Weathered terracotta, coarse woven textiles and well-worn rugs
give a relaxed feel. At night, the garden can be transformed for a
festive feel with myriads of tea lights, scented candles and hangings
of sheer fabrics in fabulous colours. In the sheltered environment,
grow exotic, fragrant plants to perfume the still air (see special plants
for sheltered gardens, page 92). If your garden is frost-free and
temperatures don't get lower than about 2 ºC (36 ºF), pelargoniums
can be left outside all year and will flower for months on end – many
will flower throughout the year if kept above about 7 ºC (45 ºF).

GET THE LOOK

- **Colours**: Bright oranges, rusty reds, midnight blue, aubergine,
  intense pinks.
- **Furniture**: Wide, flat daybeds covered with woven textiles,
  leather throws and colourful bolsters and cushions. Leather
  pouffes and cube stools. Rattan chairs and tables. Circular
  mosaic tables.

MAKE A DAYBED

Relax in your garden on
a comfortable daybed.

1 Build up a generous level
area off the ground and
against a wall using large
concrete blocks mortared in
place. Render the blocks with
a coating of smooth concrete
to achieve a flat surface.

2 Have a slim foam
mattress cut to fit (visit
a foam specialist). Cover it
with tough canvas or cotton,
stapled to the underside.

3 Cover your daybed with
rush matting, kilims
and Moroccan textiles.

LEFT BEAUTIFULLY WEATHERED
TERRACOTTA POTS MAKE A RELAXED LOOK
AND CONTAIN SPIKY YUCCAS, FRAGRANT
LAVENDER AND HOT-COLOURED ZONAL
PELARGONIUMS. THESE WILL ALL FLOURISH
IN A SHELTERED COURTYARD AND ARE
EASY TO LOOK AFTER AS THEY ARE
DROUGHT-TOLERANT (IT WON'T MATTER
IF YOU FORGET TO WATER THEM). RUSH
MATTING FEELS PLEASANT UNDERFOOT
AND HIDES UNATTRACTIVE PAVING.

ABOVE RIGHT AND RIGHT LARGE BAMBOO
VESSELS CAN BE USED TO HOLD PLANTS
IN FUNCTIONAL PLASTIC POTS, OR LOOK
GOOD SIMPLY LEFT EMPTY. SQUARE-CUT
LOGS SLOT TOGETHER TO FORM A LONG
TABLE THAT WOULD EASILY DOUBLE UP AS
A BENCH IF EXTRA SEATING WERE NEEDED.

- **Flooring**: woven rush matting and woven or leather rugs.
- **Plant containers**: natural and colourfully patterned terracotta, dark blue glazed, Ali Baba jars, long urns with handles.
- **Accessories**: carpets, tents, awnings, iron fretwork screens, candles, tea lights, metal lanterns, mosaic-framed mirrors.
- **Key plants**: palms, citrus trees, jasmine, pelargoniums, mint, gardenias, aromatic herbs.

THIS PAGE IN A SHELTERED COURTYARD, TENDER INDOOR PLANTS CAN HAVE A HOLIDAY OUTSIDE IN SUMMER MONTHS. A BEAUTIFUL CRIMSON CHINESE HIBISCUS (*HIBISCUS ROSA-SINENSIS*) AND ZONAL PELAGARONIUMS ADD AN EXOTIC TOUCH. **RIGHT** CUSHIONS COVERED WITH WOVEN RUSH AND EDGED IN PINK COTTON LINK PERFECTLY WITH THE MAGENTA PELARGONIUM AND RUSH MATTING.

MOROCCAN MINT

Why not grow pots of mint in a shady corner? The leaves can be dried for a delicious tea or used fresh in Moroccan tabbouleh salads. Mint is easy to grow (if it's not grown in a pot, it can be far too rampant), but keep the pots well watered as it likes moist soil.

SHABBY CHIC

For an easy life, don't bother with pristine or cutting-edge designs. Well-loved, worn furnishings give a comfortable, homely feel. Rummage through family attics, junk shops and flea markets for second-hand furniture and old-fashioned accessories. If you are a hoarder, this look is for you: collections of nostalgic clutter enhance the lived-in style.

GET THE LOOK

This easy, unaffected style is easy to achieve using worn and faded furnishings, with splashes of primary colour here and there on accessories or furniture to add some zest.

- **Furniture**: Old painted wooden chairs and tables (if they are chipped or flaking, so much the better). Comfortable wicker chairs. An antique iron bed would make a fun place to laze.
- **Flooring**: Wooden decking (painted or left plain), spread with threadbare floral rugs in dry weather.

- **Fabrics**: Faded floral chintz, patchwork quilts, plaid picnic rugs, cotton ticking, antique French linen, checked tablecloths.
- **Plant containers**: Floral china, enamel buckets, Cornishware, cups and jugs (if necessary, drill holes in the base for drainage).
- **Accessories**: Indoor lamps with tassled shades, piles of vintage *Vogue* magazines, glass jars for holding candles when its breezy, old decorated enamel storage tins for holding packets of seeds, string and any other odds and ends.

LEFT FLAKING PAINT AND FADED FABRICS CREATE A LAID-BACK, HOMELY FEEL. ADD CHEERFUL SPLASHES OF BRIGHT COLOUR TO FRESHEN UP THE GARDEN AND STOP THE EFFECT FROM BEING DULL OR JUST PLAIN SHABBY (WITHOUT THE CHIC).

ABOVE LEFT SILVERY COTTON LAVENDER (*SANTOLINA CHAMAECYPARISSUS*) HAS JOLLY BRIGHT YELLOM POMPOM FLOWERS AND IS DELICIOUSLY AROMATIC. BLUE LAVENDER (*LAVANDULA*) WILL TAKE OVER THE FLOWERING ONCE THE COTTON LAVENDER HAS STARTED TO FADE.

ABOVE RIGHT FUNCTIONAL CHINA IN PRETTY ICE-CREAM COLOURS TIES IN WELL WITH THE MUTED SCHEME.

ROOF TERRACES & BALCONIES

Roof terraces have become highly desirable garden rooms, and many city homeowners are now investing serious sums of money in converting their roof into a flat enclosure that they can venture out onto. Using the uppermost limits of our homes is a significant development in modern gardening. The trend makes good sense: a roof garden can be a fabulous (and generous) extra living space.

Roof terraces are a glorious mix of the false and the sublime. Making a garden on a roof is deeply artificial; after all, plants are far removed from their natural ground-level habitat. But because a roof garden is often unexpected, it is all the more delightful. To enter a building and walk up flights of stairs and then arrive in a high-level Eden with spectacular views of city and clouds, is a truly heavenly experience. The air is fresher and cleaner, there is no shade from surrounding buildings and warm sunlight can be relished. In addition, roof terraces tend to be more private than ground-floor gardens and some are completely secret hideaways. When you are not overlooked, eating out, lazing in the sun with a book or even sitting in a hot tub becomes all the more appealing.

THE PRACTICALITIES

Before you use your roof, you must determine whether it is safe to do so. It is crucial to establish its load-bearing capabilities. Consult a qualified structural engineer, who should be able to tell you what you can put on your roof (and where you can put it). Hire a reputable person, either through personal recommendation or via the appropriate association, and always get a written report. Remember that wet soil is really heavy, so do not put containers out on your roof until you know how much weight it will take. You must also take into account how many people you want to invite onto it. If you're going to hold big parties, the extra weight will be considerable. Talk to the professionals first.

Next, make sure the roof terrace is securely fenced off. The adequacy of the boundary fence should also be covered in the structural engineer's report. Check that any existing railings or walls are sturdy and safe and replace any that are not. Once the area is properly enclosed, it can provide a secure city space for children to play outside, provided they are properly supervised.

CREATING WINDBREAKS

On exposed roof gardens, you'll need some shelter from the wind. Even when the air appears to be motionless at ground level, there may be a howling gale on the roof. Solid barriers can be used to create small pockets of still air, but they tend to set up eddies of wind that whirl down the supposedly protected side of the windbreak. Permeable materials work best as these slow down the flow of the air – try trellis or wire mesh (these can both also be used to support climbing plants), or plastic webbing (used by farmers to protect crops and very effective). Alternatively, put up wooden planks to form a fence, but leave narrow gaps between them to allow air to flow through. On less-exposed terraces, solid panels can work. Rigid translucent plastic or polycarbonate sheeting supported by posts is tough and attractively modern; it is not too heavy and would maintain a high level of light.

LEFT A SMALL ROOF TERRACE CAN PROVIDE AN IDYLLIC, AND SUPRISINGLY PRIVATE, SPOT FOR MORNING COFFEE. STURDY SQUARE TRELLIS SUPPORTS A LUSH COVERING OF IVY AND WISTERIA, ALMOST BLOCKING OUT THE OUTSIDE WORLD. THE WISTERIA WILL DROP ITS LEAVES, SO PRECIOUS WINTER SUNLIGHT WILL NOT BE EXCLUDED FROM INDOORS. PRETTY PELARGONIUMS PRODUCE NON-STOP FLOWERS UNTIL THE FIRST FROSTS, WHEN THEY SHOULD BE TAKEN INSIDE.

LEFT WHEN CHOOSING FUNCTIONAL OBJECTS, YOU NEEDN'T SETTLE FOR THE MUNDANE. A TASSELLED, EMERALD SUN PARASOL WILL PROVIDE SHELTER JUST AS WELL AS ITS ORDINARY RELATIVES.

RIGHT SPIKY-LEAVED PLANTS FROM HOT COUNTRIES WORK WELL ON A ROOF: THEY LOVE SUN AND ARE GENERALLY DROUGHT TOLERANT SO THEY WON'T MIND THE DESICCATING CONDITIONS.

plants would provide lovely dappled shade, or fabric panels of tough sailcloth could be strung between metal poles (erected overhead and along the sides of the terrace) and pulled across like curtains when shelter from wind or sun, or complete privacy, is desired. Rush or split bamboo matting can make an attractive overhead or side screen. It looks pleasantly natural, and allows thin slivers of sunlight to filter through. Whole bamboo canes could be nailed to a frame to form a ceiling (a good permanent option if the roof is overlooked). Trees would also cast shade (see rooftop trees, page 61). Make sure any overhead structures are safely secured. One good solution is to weigh them down by attaching them to heavy, soil-filled planters.

FLOORING

If the roof is not too exposed, loose pea gravel could be spread over the surface; this looks great with seaside plants. Alternatively, gravel or sand could be glued in place with a resin bond to form a textured, solid surface. Decking is another good option and it can be laid over the existing roof (raise underlying joists on blocks if they might impede drainage). Decking won't be too hot to walk on in the sun and it shouldn't become slippery (except where parapet walls create areas of shade). Tiles (perhaps of terracotta or thin stone), if not too heavy, are another possibility on a roof.

CONTAINERS

Light containers are the best choice on a roof terrace: fibreglass, marine plywood, plastic or light sheet metal are all suitable options. Shiny metal would gleam beautifully in the sun. If you've already used decking as the floor surface, you could also cover cheap plastic planters or raised beds in matching wood for a streamlined look. Put a layer of appropriately light drainage material, such as chunks of polystyrene (styrofoam) or leica,

Plants can also provide great shelter from the wind, as their leaves filter the air, slowing it down. Try some of the tougher, hardier shrubs and trees, and plant a thick hedge along the windward side of the roof (see rooftop trees and tough shrubs, page 61).

When choosing your windbreak or boundaries, think about how to use solid and transparent constructions so you can create areas where you are completely hidden away while maintaining spectacular views. In all cases, include the weight of any new boundaries in your load-bearing calculations, and make sure the fences and screens are securely anchored (ideally by a professional), and won't be swept away by strong wind.

PROVIDING SHADE

You will also need some protection from the sun. Overhead structures can be temporary or permanent – a sun umbrella is an easy option, but make sure it's very firmly secured and take it down when you aren't using the roof. An arbour with climbing

in the base of your planters – this will improve drainage and will also minimize the heavy soil content. You could use special lightweight compost (potting soil) if the weight restrictions are severe. Finally, make sure any containers positioned near the edge of your roof terrace are securely anchored, particularly if they contain tall plants that might blow over in the wind.

DECORATION

Picking up details in the view and echoing them on the roof is fun. Witty effects can be achieved and the space will tie in with its surroundings; for example, the design of the railings could mimic the shape (dome, spire, crenellation) of a conspicuous nearby roof, or the colour of your cushions could echo that of a distant skyscraper. You could even paint a silhouette of the skyline on a wall or across the planting boxes. If you've got a great view of neon lights by night, instead of more conventional lighting, try installing your own neon. Choose a word or phrase that appeals to you and have it made in neon tubing.

Old chimneypots will fit in well with period buildings. You could place a row of them, safely secured, along a parapet wall for extra privacy. Sun loungers are the ultimate furniture for a roof terrace or, if you've decided on a seaside theme, deck chairs and steamer chairs would also look good.

Install a water feature to cool the air and provide a refreshing and relaxing sound. As water is very heavy, choose a small version; a mini-fountain in a metallic bowl would sparkle in the sun. Another good small option for roof-terrace water is a bubble fountain (see water, pages 126–30). Or, to make a shallow pool appear deeper, line its base with a mirror.

SUITABLE PLANTS

Grow plants that respond well to cliff-top conditions, as they need to be able to cope with strong, drying winds and hot sun. Seaside and Mediterranean plants are a good choice. Many types of herb will flourish and some of them have evergreen foliage for

year-round good looks. Try rosemary, sage, thyme, marjoram, hyssop, winter savoury and tarragon. For rooftop flowers, you could grow osteospermums, pelargoniums, gazanias (funky daisies in hot, bright colours), catmint (catnip), montbretia (*Crocosmia*) and the Dalmatian bellflower (*Campanula portenschlagiana*).

Grasses blowing in the wind on a roof can look wonderful and their swishing foliage adds drama and movement (see groovy grasses, page 152). Airy, see-through plants also work well. They can withstand constant buffeting because wind passes through them and they can be used to frame spectacular views. Try fennel (purple, bronze or green) and purple-flowered *Verbena bonariensis*. If you want bamboo on your roof terrace, choose carefully. Most bamboos prefer humid, still air and they won't be happy on a windy rooftop. Try tougher varieties like fountain bamboo (*Fargesia nitida*) and large-leaved Japanese bamboo (*Pseudosasa japonica*).

For a minimalist look, use only dwarf or slow-growing pines. Many of these can cope with terrific winds, eventually forming fantastic, contorted shapes. The Corsican pine (*Pinus nigra* subsp. *laricio*), the dwarf mountain pine (*Pinus mugo* 'Gnom') and the dwarf Scots pine (*Pinus sylvestris* 'Watereri') are extremely tolerant of windy conditions. They would look superb with furniture and planters made of rough-hewn, dark brown-stained wood and plain, monochrome flooring. To create a Zen look, add raked grey gravel and a few carefully chosen rocks.

To maintain your plants, it is essential to install a good watering system. Even when it's not sunny, windy conditions can be very desiccating and carrying heavy watering cans up to the roof would not be fun (see irrigation, page 136).

BALCONIES

As balconies share many of the characteristics of roof terraces, the same design considerations often apply. The great advantage of a balcony is that they are built to enhance the interior (a roof terrace is often an afterthought), so they tend to be easily accessible and

ROOFTOP TREES

On larger roof gardens, trees are valuable for their height. They make a flat roof look more interesting, cast welcome shade and provide smaller plants with protection from wind and sun. Suitable trees include:

- Silver birch (*Betula pendula*) and Himalayan birch (*Betula utilis*): The variety *jacquemontii* has lovely white bark.
- Holly (*Ilex aquifolium*): Hollies are evergreen; some types have silver- or gold-variegated leaves.
- Hawthorn (*Crataegus monogyna*) or *C. laevigata*: 'Paul's Scarlet' has dark pink flowers.
- Strawberry tree (*Arbutus unedo*): This is evergreen.
- Mountain ash (*Sorbus aucuparia*): Decorative orange-red berries.
- Whitebeam (*Sorbus aria*) 'Lutescens': Eye-catching silvered leaves.
- Pine (*Pinus*): Evergreen; dwarf varieties are particularly suitable for a roof garden.

LEFT *VERBENA BONARIENSIS* IS AN EXCELLENT PLANT, WITH TALL BRANCHING STEMS THAT BEAR DENSE CLUSTERS OF PURPLE-PINK FLOWERS IN LATE SUMMER AND AUTUMN. IT HAS AN AIRY, 'SEE-THROUGH' STRUCTURE AND GIVES HEIGHT WITHOUT BEING CUMBERSOME.

TOUGH SHRUBS

Some shrubs are tough enough to be used as effective windbreaks on a roof terrace. You could use the following:

- Sea buckthorn (*Hippophae rhamnoides*): This has silvery leaves; if male plants are grown close by, female plants will produce orange berries.
- *Elaeagnus x ebbingei*: A robust evergreen with dark green metallic leaves with silvery-beige undersides. Mature plants produce tiny autumn flowers with a sweet penetrating fragrance.
- Purple barberry (*Berberis x ottawensis* 'Superba'): A thorny deciduous shrub with small purple leaves and yellow spring flowers.
- Common elder (*Sambucus nigra*): Fast-growing and deciduous. 'Guincho Purple' has marvellous purple leaves. Avoid golden varieties on a rooftop as they will scorch.
- Privet (*Ligustrum vulgare*): This is not a great beauty, but it is fast-growing and tough. It has dark green leaves and small white flowers.
- Laurustinus (*Viburnum tinus*): This has evergreen dark leaves and clusters of white flowers in winter and spring.

visible from inside. Treat your balcony as an extension of your inside room and decorate it in a similar style. For example, you could use the same flooring outside as you have used inside (on a small balcony this should not be prohibitively expensive). Linking indoors and out will benefit both spaces – the balcony will feel like part of the home and both will seem larger. You could also use the same paint colour inside and out, or use the same containers, furniture or accessories to extend the effect.

Balconies are usually much smaller than roof terraces but, even on a tiny balcony, try to incorporate seating or at least leave room so you can carry a chair outside (you will enjoy and use it far more). There are a few space-saving tricks that are worth considering, too. Use flat-backed containers (rather than round pots) to fit neatly along the edges of your balcony. Hang containers on walls or on top of the railings to preserve precious floor space and, if you want a water feature, go for a wall-mounted fountain. A box bench is a good choice of seating: it fits snugly up against a wall

and will accommodate a few people. It also doubles up to provide a handy storage space for a watering can, plant food, a trowel and gardening gloves (essential kit even if you've only got a few plants).

Balconies are often less private than roof terraces. You could put a screen along one side to create some privacy, but don't box the whole space in; luxuriate in the view instead. If there's another balcony directly above, yours won't get much rain, so you'll need to be extra vigilant about watering. A balcony will be seen all year round, so grow some evergreen plants to stop it looking bare in winter; those with fragrant flowers offer an added bonus. If your balcony is on the sunny side of the building, an awning would be useful; make one in a fabric that ties in with your interior decoration.

Balconies are often long and narrow, so place a focal point, such as a spiky plant or sculpture at one end to draw the eye along the space. To make it seem wider, lay flooring so the boards run across the balcony, rather than down its length. Your balcony probably already has railings around it. Consider whether they could be improved: a lick of paint might work wonders, or you could commission customized railings in a fabulous contemporary design to replace them altogether.

As with roof terraces, the load-bearing capability and the stability and adequacy of the fencing should be established through a proper structural survey. Weight restrictions on balconies are often even greater than on roof terraces, since balconies usually hang off the side of a building. Don't use your balcony until you are sure it's completely safe. Make sure railings are totally secure and that they will contain small children.

LEFT LIGHTWEIGHT FOLDING TABLES AND CHAIRS AND CANVAS SUN UMBRELLAS ARE EXCELLENT OPTIONS ON A TINY BALCONY – THEY CAN BE STACKED AWAY NEATLY AGAINST A WALL WHEN YOU WANT TO FREE UP THE SPACE.

RIGHT READY-MADE SQUARES OF DECKING CAN EASILY BE SLOTTED TOGETHER TO HIDE AN UGLY BALCONY FLOOR. EITHER CUT THEM TO FIT AWKWARD CORNERS OR FILL GAPS WITH SHINGLE, COBBLESTONES OR CRUSHED STONE.

SILVER AND BLUE PLANTS

Silver and blue-leaved plants shimmer in the sun and look fabulous together. Many of them come from the Mediterranean or other coastal regions and they will thrive in the sun on a roof.

- Artemisias: An array of amazingly silvery plants. *A. alba* 'Canescens' has contorted coral-like leaves. *A.* 'Powis Castle' produces clouds of filigree foliage. *A. stelleriana* 'Boughton Silver' is silvery white.
- *Euphorbia characias* subsp. *wulfenii*: This has blue-green leaves in ruffles around its stems, and long-lasting rounded heads of lime-green flowers.
- Sea hollies (*Eryngium*) (above right): Spectacular thistle-like plants with spiky flower heads that range from extraordinarily bright blue (*E. bourgatii* 'Oxford Blue') through silvery-white (Miss Willmott's Ghost, *E. giganteum*) to steel and mauve (*E. amethystinum*).
- Cotton lavender (*Santolina chamaecyparissus*): This has tiny, aromatic silver-grey leaves dotted with yellow pompom flowers in summer. It can be clipped into a neat ball.

- Houseleeks (*Sempervivum*): Gorgeous, small succulent rosettes, ranging from blue-green to red, and some are decorated with intricate 'cobwebs'. Extremely tough, they can even survive without soil and are evergreen.
- Lavender (*Lavandula stoechas* subsp. *pedunculata*) (far right): Silvery bushes with spikes of fragrant flowers. Not all lavenders are violet-blue; look for pink, purple and white varieties, too.
- Blue fescue (*Festuca glauca*) (below right): A densely tufted, evergreen grass with spiky, blue leaves. The variety 'Blaufuchs' has the brightest blue leaves.
- Ice plant (*Sedum spectabile*): Attractive, fleshy grey-green leaves and long-lasting, flat clumps of tiny flowers.
- Marguerite (margarita) (*Argyranthemum gracile* 'Chelsea Girl'): Pretty white daisies with yellow centres and dainty, thread-like grey-green foliage. It should be taken into a cool room if frosts threaten.
- *Convolvulus cneorum*: A rounded evergreen bush with silky silver leaves. Its elegant white flowers bloom for several months.

CHINESE ORIENTAL

Although Japan has a well-known and distinctive tradition of garden design, Eastern-style decor needn't draw its influences solely from there – a Chinese theme could also be used to create a wonderfully exotic garden room. Use patterned silks, glazed pots, tiles and statues, paper lanterns, miniature pagodas, bamboo, intricately carved dragons and wind chimes. Choose plants that have an allegorical significance in Chinese gardens: peach (*Prunus persica*) symbolizes immortality; water lily (*Nymphaea*) purity and truth; the jointed stems of bamboo symbolize the steps along the path to enlightenment; magnolia symbolizes gentleness and beauty; and cherry (*Prunus* varieties) spring and youth. Other popular flowers include peonies, day lilies, orchids and tiger lilies.

Bamboo cane can instantly create an oriental feel and its natural golden brown tones fit in well outdoors. In addition, it is often cheaper to use bamboo than natural wood. Bamboo is an amazingly versatile material, with a wide range of products, from flooring, fencing and screens to chairs, loungers, tables, wind chimes, plant supports and plant holders.

Thick canes can be used whole for a strong fence (pushed into the ground like fencing posts and lashed together) or sturdy furniture, while short sections can make plant holders (simply drop your pot plant into the hollow stem). Thick bamboo can also be sawn lengthways to form flattish struts, as for the floor tiles, deck chair and day bed on this roof terrace. Slim bamboo canes give a more delicate effect. They could be nailed to an overhead frame for a light, semi-transparent screen that will create attractive barred shadows and provide privacy on an overlooked terrace. Bamboo is also available split into very thin pieces and made into rolls of matting, which is great for flooring, decorating walls and fences or attaching overhead. Ask about availability at your garden centre or try mail-order garden decor catalogues.

FENG SHUI

To perfect an oriental design, you could call in a feng shui consultant to organize your outdoor room so the ch'i, or energy, can flow freely through it, rather than unhealthily accelerate or stagnate. As a basic principle, ch'i likes to flow in curves, so there should be no straight edges to any of the main garden features like the ponds and paths. Avoid narrow paths or openings which will cause the ch'i to flow too fast and place lights or water in dark corners to prevent the ch'i becoming stuck in them.

LEFT CHINESE PAPER LANTERNS AND BRIGHT SILK CUSHIONS PROVIDE SPLASHES OF COLOUR AGAINST A BACKDROP OF BAMBOO AND LEAFY GREEN. A PINKISH ICE PLANT (*SEDUM SPECTABILE* 'SEPTEMBERGLUT') WILL FLOURISH IN THE FULL SUN ON A ROOF.

ABOVE IF YOU ARE PLANNING TO ENTERTAIN ON YOUR ROOF, MAKE IT A MEMORABLE EVENT BY DRESSING THE SPACE UP. A SPECTACULAR ORCHID IS STRICTLY A HOUSEPLANT BUT, AS A TEMPORARY VISITOR, IT FITS IN BEAUTIFULLY WITH EASTERN-STYLE DECOR.

RIGHT A LENGTH OF PRETTILY PATTERNED FABRIC CAN BE LOOPED UP OVERHEAD TO BILLOW PRETTILY IN GENTLE BREEZES AND GIVE A SENSE OF ENCLOSURE.

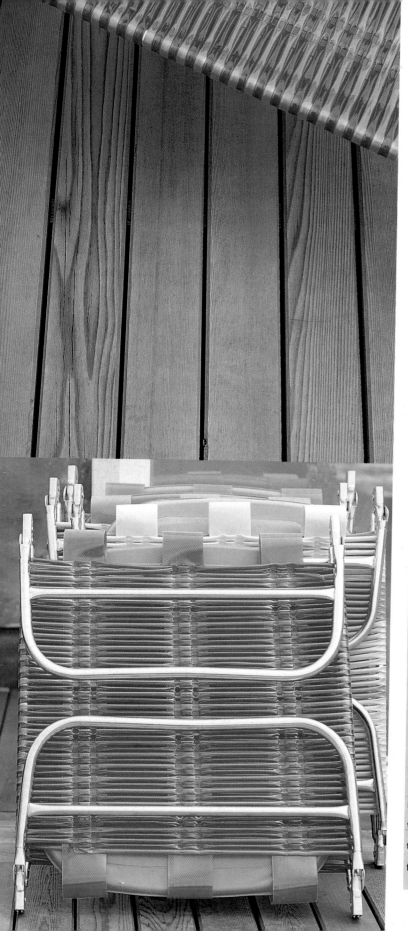

MIAMI ROOFTOP

For a fresh, fun space think Florida and kit your garden out with cheerful tropical colours and a selection of funky and spiky hot-country plants (in temperate climates, indoor plants can enjoy a summer break outside in warm weather). Palms, cabbage palms (*Cordyline australis*) and yuccas all evoke blazing hot sun and fit the look (see jungle plants, pages 142–3, and super spiky plants, page 35). Taller palm trees could be a good investment if you've got a large roof, giving the planting variety in height and providing some valuable shade. For bright splashes of long-lasting blooms, look for summer-flowering annuals and tender plants with iridescent flowers, such as begonias, busy lizzies (*Impatiens* – the New Guinea hybrids are particularly brazen), dahlias and gazanias. Succulent plants with fleshy leaves thrive in sun and add to the tropical feel: try aloes, century plants (*Agave americana*), aeoniums (*Aeonium arboreum* 'Atropurpureum' has wicked purple leaves), echeverias and jade plants (*Crassula ovata*). All are frost tender.

WISTERIA: ALL YOU NEED TO KNOW

Wisteria flaunts long tassels of fragrant flowers in blue, violet, pink or white and is easy to grow. It makes a wonderful canopy over a pergola or a spectacular adornment on a wall. Chinese wisteria (*Wisteria sinensis*) is a rampant climber, so grow Japanese wisteria (*Wisteria floribunda*) in a small space as it's more controllable. Wisteria is happiest in full sun, but it tolerates shade. It needs to be properly pruned to flower really well. Cut all side shoots back to five or six buds (leaf joints) from the main stem in mid-summer. Cut back further to two or three buds in late winter. A mature wisteria will become very heavy, so grow it on a strong support and not flimsy wooden trellis. It can take a while to flower (five years is common), though a grafted plant, rather than a seed-raised variety, will flower from a younger age. It is deciduous, but the twisted and gnarled bare stems of older plants are a wonderful winter feature. It likes rich, moist soil and is best grown on a sheltered wall to protect its flower buds from frost damage. It can also be trained as a tree-like standard.

GET THE LOOK

- **Colours**: Loud, bright and showy. Carmine, orange, pink, cobalt, yellow, lime green and pure white.
- **Furniture**: Anything in slinky white plastic or Perspex. Coloured plastic loungers, chrome and white nylon chairs and loungers.
- **Flooring**: Decking, woven plastic mats, play sand.
- **Finishing touches**: Install a drinks bar (complete with kitsch cocktail glasses and swizzle sticks) and get down to the serious business of being a glamorous film-star type.

LEFT A TWO-TONE PINK *SEMPERFLORENS* BEGONIA STRIKES JUST THE RIGHT GAUDY-BUT-PRETTY NOTE.

ABOVE LEFT A SINUOUS WHITE TABLE-COME-SUN LOUNGER IS PERFECT FOR A MIAMI-STYLE ROOFTOP. IT CAN FULFIL SEVERAL FUNCTIONS IN THE LIMITED

SPACE AND, AS IT'S PLASTIC, IT CAN BE LEFT OUTDOORS. IN THE ABSENCE OF SOIL, IT SHOULD REMAIN BEAUTIFULLY WHITE.

ABOVE RIGHT A SPIKY ALOE VERA ENJOYS THE WARM WEATHER ON A TERRACE, BUT IT MUST BE TAKEN IN IF TEMPERATURES DROP BELOW 10 ºC (50 ºF).

SUPER STRIPY POTS

Dreary plastic or cheap terracotta pots can be spiced up with a bit of imagination and some paint. Rather than painting just one or two, do a selection for a strong and coherent statement. You will need three paint colours for each colour scheme – you could use tester pots.

1 Make sure the pot is clean and dry. Paint the outside of the pot with a base coat of the lightest colour. (Painting the base and inside is optional; a chink of terracotta inside the rim and at the bottom of the pot might look good.)

2 Paint bands of the second colour around the pot – do one or two narrow bands at the top and a broad band around the middle. Around the base, paint another broad band or one or two narrow bands.

3 Paint a band or two of the accent third colour over the broad bands of the second colour and around the top or base of the pot.

4 Varnish over the areas you have painted with exterior-grade varnish.

NORTHERN SHORE

Take inspiration from the seashore and northern Scandinavia and design a futuristic seaside garden. Muted colours and unusual materials can create a stark, almost post-nuclear, effect on a tiny urban balcony. Uncompromising design makes a strong impact in a small space, but the balcony remains a useful outdoor room where quiet moments can be spent mulling over the cityscape.

Avoid the usual green-leaved plants and create a sombre, modern effect with bronze- or black-leaved plants. Some types of New Zealand flax (*Phormium tenax*) have bronze foliage; look for the dwarf 'Bronze Baby' and stripy 'Sundowner'. Bronze fennel (*Foeniculum vulgare* 'Giant Bronze') has feathery foliage and is pungently aromatic. Stonecrop (*Sedum* subsp. *maximum* 'Atropurpureum') has fleshy, dark purple-brown leaves, whereas small black lilyturf (*Ophiopogon planiscapus* 'Nigrescens') has strappy, almost black leaves. For a larger plant, use the fast-growing blackish-purple elder (*Sambucus nigra* 'Guincho Purple').

GET THE LOOK

- **Flooring**: Recall the seashore with water-worn pea shingle and cobblestones. Plastic tiles with a 'cobbled' pattern are an amusing alternative and better for walking or standing furniture on.
- **Furniture**: Smooth cast concrete has a bleak, modern look (but can still be very comfortable). Ceramic 'boulders' and modern, pared-down designs in natural wood (avoid traditional designs).
- **Accessories**: Scandinavian carved natural wood (organic and abstract shapes work well). Found objects like pieces of driftwood or rusting cans could make interesting features; you could use them as unusual plant containers.

LEFT SHINGLE AND COBBLESTONES EVOKE THE SEA SHORE, AND NEW ZEALAND FLAX (*PHORMIUM TENAX* 'BRONZE BABY') FITS IN WITH THE MUTED TONES. ABSTRACT WOOD SCULPTURES AND A CAST CONCRETE SEAT GIVE A FIRMLY MODERN FEEL.

ABOVE LEFT A FUTURISTIC WATERING CAN TIES IN WITH THE LOOK AND BRINGS A NOTE OF HUMOUR.

ABOVE RIGHT CREATE YOUR OWN ORGANIC SCULPTURES BY STACKING BEAUTIFUL WATER-WORN STONES.

BASEMENTS & LIGHT WELLS

Many city homes have no outside space other than a basement or light well. Usually ignored, they can be extremely uninviting. Their main characteristics are lack of light, high walls (making the sky seem very far away), and motionless, damp, perhaps rather stultifying air. But use these negative elements to your advantage and you can have a jewel of a garden.

THE WALLS

Exploit the vertical surfaces and use them to create the illusion of sunlight. To brighten up the space, paint them in an off-white or pale colour (pure white can look rather stark and unnatural outdoors). Put brushed aluminium, zinc or stainless-steel panels on walls; they will reflect light without giving clear reflections. If you can site a mirror so that it isn't immediately obvious (you don't want to come face to face with your reflection when you look outside), use one to increase the light levels and create an illusion of greater space.

If you leave high walls bare, the space will feel claustrophobic and closed in. To make walls appear less overwhelming, break up their surface visually by decorating them, or counterbalance them with horizontal structures. Overhead structures also detract from high walls and create a more intimate living space, but avoid using solid or heavy constructions over a basement garden. Thin wires, ropes, wooden strips or bamboo canes put up overhead would be sufficient to define the space and won't cut out precious natural light. Sparse and delicate climbers could be grown along them.

Alleviate soaring walls by painting horizontal stripes across them or by attaching trellis to them. Dispel the gloom by painting the trellis a bright colour: yellow would be invigorating. Perspective trellis can add depth and make a space seem larger; arches and rectangles are widely available. Avoid applying trellis to every available surface, though, or your garden could resemble a birdcage!

If you've got some spare cash, you could commission a mural. Indulge in a flight of fancy with a scene of classical temples and distant mountains, or wild-eyed tigers skulking through a tropical rainforest. A trompe l'oeil mural (designed to create an illusion and trick the eye) can give the impression of a greater space. And, of course, murals look good in winter when plants may have lost their leaves. You could contact the art department of your local college to see whether a student would be interested in taking on the work. (Ask to see their portfolio first.) The quality needn't be fantastic outdoors and you might get a masterpiece.

High walls mean plenty of space to grow climbers. Go for those that tolerate shade and have good foliage, as many climbers only bear their flowers at the top where you won't see much of them. If you don't want trellis or wires, choose self-clinging climbers (see climbers for shady gardens, page 86, and easy climbers, page 142).

You could also decorate plain walls with lattice panels (perhaps in wicker or wrought iron) or matting (try split bamboo or rush). To keep limited floor space free and add height, put up shelves (place pots of plants or decorative objects on them or use them for extra storage); their horizontal lines will help break up a vertical sweep of wall. Pot holders can also be attached to walls, and wall pots are designed so they can be hung without a holder.

LEFT A COAT OF PAINT IS A SIMPLE WAY TO GIVE A DRAB BASEMENT A LIFT. THIS DREARY OUTLOOK HAS BEEN TRANSFORMED BY PAINTING THE DIFFERENT SURFACES A UNIFYING, PRETTY COLOUR. CURTAINS IN A SIMILAR SHADE FRAME THE VIEW OUTSIDE, AND CHIC GLAZED PLANTERS IN PASTEL COLOURS ADD TO THE FRESH, BRIGHT FEEL.

LEFT BEAT THE GLOOM AND HIDE EXISTING UNATTRACTIVE OR DRAB PAVING WITH PALE PLASTIC FLOORING. SIMPLY ROLL IT OUT, CUT IT TO FIT AND GLUE IT DOWN IF NECESSARY. WHEN IT GETS TATTY, REPLACE IT WITH A FRESH COLOUR – PERHAPS LILAC OR TURQUOISE NEXT TIME.

RIGHT AND BELOW RIGHT FLOURISHING SHADE-LOVING PLANTS AND WHITE-PAINTED FURNITURE AND PLANT HOLDERS STOP A BASEMENT FROM LOOKING DINGY OR DULL. THE HUGE-LEAVED CASTOR OIL PLANT (*FATSIA JAPONICA*) WILL LOOK GLOSSILY HEALTHY EVEN IN DEEP SHADE.

THE FLOOR

Once you have organized the vertical surfaces, get to work at ground level. Any soil in a below-ground basement garden is probably of poor quality, so you may be better off paving or decking the area and growing all your plants in containers. Work out whether any existing paving can be retained. It may be possible to improve it with a coat or two of masonry paint (Ugly grey concrete could be totally transformed when painted a cool, pale green, for example. See page 27.) Alternatively, it might provide a suitable base for new flooring. If you do lay new flooring, use something pale. A good solution would be to use the same flooring as the inside adjoining room to link the indoor and outdoor spaces and make each seem larger.

Shiny galvanized steel or zinc containers would help to brighten up the atmosphere. Even in a basement, it's worth installing an irrigation system to water your containers unless the space is really damp and shady (see irrigation, page 136).

THE PLANTS

In dark basements and light wells, make sure you grow shade-loving plants. Without sun, most plants won't flower well, so concentrate on plants with beautiful foliage. Experiment with different shapes, textures and shades of green for a lush, subterranean paradise (see plants with great green leaves, page 147). One advantage of a basement garden (particularly one in a city) is that they tend to be sheltered from wind and, hopefully, frost. Capitalize on this by growing more delicate, exotic plants that would not survive in exposed locations. But choose those that will tolerate the light levels in your basement. Start off with the lady palm (*Rhapis excelsa*), which should cope with severe gloom.

Use a fair proportion of evergreens for year-round greenery (see shade-tolerant evergreens, page 85). Some have glossy leaves which bounce the light around and brighten up dull spaces, such as the huge-leaved castor oil plant (*Fatsia japonica*), holly (*Ilex*), Mexican orange (*Choisya ternata*), wild ginger (*Asarum*) and camellias.

Ferns are fantastic in the shade; some are evergreen, while others die down in winter. Most of them need damp soil, so don't let them dry out for long periods. Maidenhair ferns (*Adiantum*) have dainty fronds, the hart's tongue fern (*Asplenium scolopendrium*) is evergreen, and you can get it with smooth, wavy, frayed or curly leaf margins. The Japanese painted fern (*Athyrium niponicum*) is an unusual, silvery colour and the shuttlecock fern (*Matteuccia struthiopteris*) has exuberant clumps of upright fronds in the shape of a shuttlecock. In really grim conditions, use the male fern (*Dryopteris filix-mas*). It's the toughest of them all and can even cope with dry soil. There are masses of other types of fern. If your

Christmas box (*Sarcococca*) and honeysuckle (*Lonicera*). A number of lilies can cope with some shade, so it's worth giving them a try. They should flower well for the first year at least. If you want flowers, get plants that do bloom in shade, don't waste your efforts with sun-lovers (see flowers in the shade, page 91).

For extra flowers, plant bulbs between your existing plants (even in pots there's enough room to squeeze in a few snowdrops). Cyclamen, snowdrops, winter aconites and bluebells can all be used in shady gardens. If it's very shady, the bulbs may not flower so well the following year, but they can always be replaced.

When your outdoor space is so dark and shady that little more than a few leafy ferns can survive in it, use sculpture or other art as decoration instead of plants. This is also a good idea if the space is difficult to access, making plant-tending difficult. Sculpture can either be used as a focal point in the garden or placed on top of a wall to draw the eye up to the sky.

garden is in deep, deep shade, it might be fun to visit a specialist fern nursery to see all the different options – at least it would be a rare occasion when you could indulge in any plant on offer.

Other lovely plants suitable for the shade include Solomon's seal (elegant arching stems bearing white flowers and then black berries), dwarf bamboo (*Sasa veitchii*), *Arum italicum* (the variety called 'Marmoratum' has beautiful marbled leaves and will be quite happy under a deciduous shrub or tree), primroses, bleeding heart (*Dicentra*), foxgloves, mint (one of the few herbs to tolerate shade) and honesty (or money plant, *Lunaria*), which self-seeds easily.

FRAGRANT & FLOWERY SHADE

Grow deliciously scented plants – their fragrance will be caught in the still air and you'll really be able to appreciate it. This is particularly valuable when the air is dank. Who wants to hang out in a garden that doesn't smell good? Scrumptious-smelling shade dwellers include lily of the valley (*Convallaria*), mahonia, daphne,

LIGHTING

Make the most of natural light by bringing down the sky and creating reflections of the clouds. Tilt a mirror skywards or install a dark pool (use a black liner or dye the water black) for fantastic reflections on the surface. Where there's little natural light, use artificial light instead. This is particularly valuable near the house, as it can improve the atmosphere indoors, too. By day, it can be used to supplement daylight and take away dreary greyness. At night, the space can be illuminated to glow invitingly. Underwater lighting in a pool casts up a mysterious glow, heightening the atmosphere of an exotic underworld. Or, the space could be filled with a profusion of candles for a festive effect in the still night air.

ABOVE CANDLES ARE A PRACTICAL OPTION IN A SHELTERED BASEMENT. A MIRROR-MOSAIC CANDLE HOLDER MAGNIFIES THE FLICKERING LIGHT AND ENLIVENS THE SPACE WITH ITS SPARKLE.

RIGHT TRANSFORM A TINY BASEMENT INTO A LUXURIOUS OUTDOOR BOUDOIR WITH AN EXTRAVAGANT RUCHED CANOPY, BIG SQUASHY CUSHIONS AND CANDLES IN GLASS STORM LANTERNS.

FLORAL KITSCH

A kitsch look is funky, young and not too serious. Indulge in colourful, exuberant, frivolous (or even faintly farcical) kitsch to brighten up a dark or unremarkable outside space and to provide a light-hearted and ironic take on gardening. This may not be a long-term or permanent solution for your outdoor room, but you can enjoy it while it lasts and throw it away when you've had enough. It's cheap, cheerful and easy – so think plastic, think glitzy and have fun.

GET THE LOOK

- **Colours**: Anything bright, lurid or clashing, although pink reigns supreme. Shiny silver and pure white also strike the right note.
- **Flooring**: Use instant modern flooring to roll out over existing paving. Choose between plastic, lino, rubber or (most kitsch of all) astroturf, and change it to match this season's flip-flops. For underfoot luxury, take out shag-pile rugs in dry weather.
- **Furniture**: Hunt for throwaway, quirky and unashamedly glitzy or gaudy furniture. Perspex or plastic creates the look; blow-up plastic lilos and armchairs are perfect.
- **Fabrics**: Nylon, vinyl-covered cotton, plastic mesh, fake fur, anything fluffy and anything printed with vivid-coloured daisies.
- **Accessories**: Glittery mosaic balls, colourful plastic glasses, plates and cutlery, cuddly toys (very Jeff Koons), plastic or beaded door curtains, gnomes, nymph or shepherdess statues, plastic cushions, fairy lights and a blow-up paddling pool full of plastic fish.
- **Plants**: Plastic flowers, anything fake or over the top, gerberas and fluffy mop-head hydrangeas (*Hydrangea macrophylla*).

STYLE TIP

If growing your own flowers seems like too much hard work (and, in any case, they don't grow well in your shady basement), decorate your garden with colourful floral accessories, everlasting plastic flowers or fresh cut flowers.

THIS PAGE LIGHT, FOLD-UP CHAIRS CAN EASILY BE CARRIED INTO THE GARDEN FOR A DRINK ALFRESCO. A VASE OF SUMPTUOUS PINK HYDRANGEAS AND PRETTY FLORAL HANGINGS LOOK FABULOUS AGAINST A BACKDROP OF LUSH FOLIAGE AND BLUE-PAINTED WALLS. EVEN IF YOU DON'T REALLY NEED THEM, FLIP-FLOPS AND A SUN HAT WILL MAKE YOU FEEL AS IF YOU'RE IN THE SUN.

SHADE-TOLERANT EVERGREENS

Use easy evergreen plants to furnish your garden, even in the depths of winter.

- Skimmias: Easy-to-grow compact bushes. *S. reevesiana* has sealing-wax red berries; *S. japonica* 'Rubella' has clusters of tiny red buds.

- Laurustinus (*Viburnum tinus*): Very easy shrub with dark green leaves and clusters of little white flowers throughout winter and spring.

- Hellebores: The stinking hellebore (*Helleborus foetidus*) and the Corsican hellebore (*Helleborus argutifolius*) have jagged dark green leaves and exotic pale green flowers.

- *Pachysandra terminalis*: Low-growing plant that is great for covering bare soil in shade.

- *Liriope muscari*: Produces clumps of grassy leaves and spikes of purple flowers in autumn. The white-flowering type is harder to find.

- Elephant's ears (*Bergenia*): Ground-covering plants with huge, round, leathery leaves. They provide a good foil for small- or narrow-leaved plants.

- *Euonymus* 'Silver Queen': Small bush with green and white-splashed leaves, which can climb if it has support.

- Periwinkle (*Vinca*): Sprawling plant that spreads across the ground, bearing pretty purple, blue or white flowers. Some varieties are very invasive.

- Castor oil plant (*Fatsia japonica*) (below right): Fabulous big shrub with huge glossy leaves and clusters of creamy flowers, followed by their black berries; it tolerates deep gloom.

- *Mahonia japonica*: Tough, exceptionally shade-tolerant, spiky shrub with the advantage of powerfully fragrant, yellow winter flowers.

- Mexican orange blossom (*Choisya ternata*): Tolerates some shade and grows to a medium-sized, rounded bush bearing starry, delicately scented white flowers. The type called 'Sundance' has lurid, yellowish leaves, while 'Aztec Pearl' has narrow, dark green leaves.

- Wild ginger (*Asarum europaeum*): This will form a carpet on the ground and has neat, kidney-shaped leaves.

Other shade-tolerant evergreens include: Mrs Robb's bonnet (*Euphorbia amygdaloides* var. *robbiae*), which tolerates deep shade and dry soil but is invasive; box, which can be clipped; yew, which is poisonous; holly and London pride (*Saxifraga x urbium*).

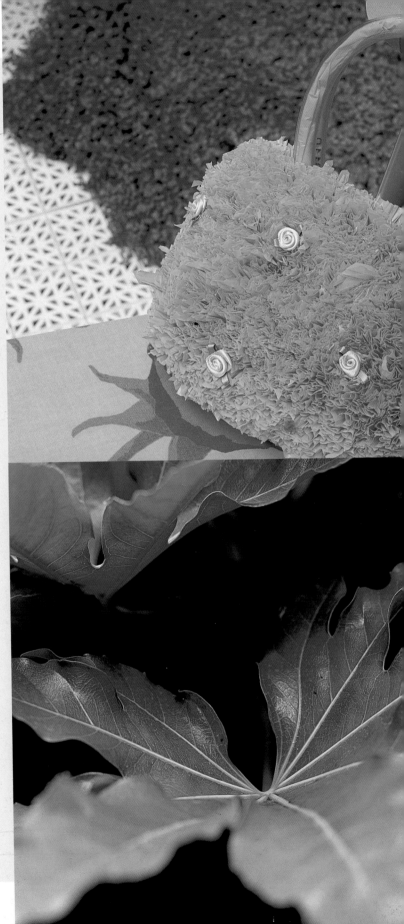

OPULENCE

A garden needn't be a simple or frugal place just because it's outdoors and exposed to the elements. For a change (or perhaps if you're planning to entertain), deck it out temporarily with lavish indoor furnishings for some open-air splendour. Make sure the weather forecast is good or get a sheet of tarpaulin which can be hooked up quickly for overhead protection while you carry all your treasures back indoors.

As long as you don't mind the upheaval, an opulent effect can easily be created in your outdoor room. Elaborate and ornate

CLIMBERS FOR
SHADY GARDENS

- Ivy (*Hedera*): The easiest climber to grow in shade, as it tolerates the deepest gloom. Use gold- or silver-splashed varieties for mock dappled sunlight. It is evergreen and self-clinging.
- Climbing hydrangea (*Hydrangea anomala* subsp. *petiolaris*): This has pretty clusters of white summer flowers and is deciduous with brown-red stems. It grows slowly at first, but becomes self-clinging.
- Honeysuckle (*Lonicera*): Scrambling climbers that give a wild, informal feel. Some have a fabulous scent.
- Virginia creeper (*Parthenocissus quinquefolia*), Chinese Virginia creeper (*Parthenocissus henryana*) and Boston ivy (*Parthenocissus*

tricuspidata): These are all easy-to-grow, self-clinging, deciduous climbers with leaves that turn spectacular colours in the autumn before they drop. They can be used to quickly cover a large wall, but may be difficult to control in a small space. The Chinese type is more manageable than other varieties.

- Clematis: Some varieties can cope with moderate shade, although they will climb towards the light and flower mainly at the top. Try *Clematis alpina* and *Clematis tangutica*.
- Chocolate vine (*Akebia quinata*) or Chilean bellflower (*Lapageria rosea*): Try either of these for something a bit more exotic. They will both tolerate some shade and the latter likes acid soil.

furnishings and accessories really stand out in the unpolished, natural setting provided by the garden (a Louis Quinze sofa that you may not even notice in the corner of a comfortable living room will certainly catch the eye out of doors). The incongruity of what is clearly indoor furniture being outside gives the look its impact.

GET THE LOOK

- Hunt around indoors for any lavish or ornate pieces of furniture that you could easily take outside. Don't get carried away and take too much out; if you have a few friends coming round for supper, just make sure there's a place for everyone to sit. If your furniture is all streamlined chrome, abandon the idea or cover it with luxurious or intricately patterned fabrics.
- Carry out and carefully position your chosen furniture. In a larger garden, choose a suitable corner or terrace to decorate. Arrange the furniture as you would in an indoor room. Add cushions for extra comfort and spread plenty of throws and blankets around for sybaritic luxury.

- Dress up the space by hanging pretty fabrics or throws over the walls and spreading rugs on the floor (put down plastic sheets first to protect them). You could even hang pictures or mirrors (preferably gilt or gold-framed ones) on the garden walls.
- Hang up a chandelier for splendid lighting (get one that takes candles so you can use it outdoors) and place candles in elegant glass storm lanterns on tables and along walls.
- Select glassware and china to tie in with the look – the more gilt, the better. If you've got any Victorian-style urns, these would look great standing nearby. A pretty fake plant or fabulous cut flowers can be added for decoration.

THIS PAGE AND PREVIOUS PAGE
AGAINST THE UNPRETENTIOUS BACKDROP OF A ROUGH BRICK WALL AND COMMON IVY (*HEDERA HELIX*), ORNATE ANTIQUE FURNITURE (PARTICULARLY DIVANS AND CHAISES LONGUES FOR DISSOLUTE LOUNGING), A FLAMBOYANT CHANDELIER AND A TASSLED SILK SHAWL CREATE AN OPULENT ATMOSPHERE. THE BAROQUE WALL SCULPTURE SEEMS TO GAZE DOWN APPRECIATIVELY AT THIS IDEAL SPOT FOR SQUANDERING A LAZY AFTERNOON.

MEDITERRANEAN

A Mediterranean style gives a warm and inviting feel to a garden and is evocative of sunny climes and a relaxed pace of life. Olive and fig trees, vine-covered pergolas and rustic terracotta pots are all redolent of the Mediterranean region. Natural stone walls and cobbled or terracotta-tiled terraces would look wonderful (if you can afford them). Alternatively, use gravel or imitation terracotta pavers for paths and terraces, and improve unattractive walls with plaster and masonry paint. Brighten up gloomy gardens by white-washing the walls or use natural, earth-coloured tones (try shades of ochre, umber and sienna) or pretty pastel colours. As a finishing touch, walls could be topped with large terracotta pan tiles.

For this style, the garden does not need to be immaculate: peeling paint, distressed wooden or metal furniture and sprawling herbs all create an easygoing atmosphere. Colourful flowers and crisp fabrics (such as Provençal cotton tablecloths or cushions) will prevent the overall effect from appearing shabby. Group attractive containers on terraces and window ledges (weathered terracotta or glazed azure-blue ceramic would suit the look). You could build a plant-festooned pergola over a rustic table and chairs for a lovely place to eat outside. In climates with cold, grey winters, grow deciduous climbers over the pergola if it's near the house. The leaves will fall in autumn, so precious winter sunlight won't be lost indoors. Vines, wisteria and Virginia creeper are all suitable options. Honey-coloured gravel could be spread over bare soil between your plants for a warm effect and to keep weeds down. Finally, in a sheltered garden, you could plant highly fragrant jasmine and vivid bougainvilleas, and position clipped bay trees to frame the doorway.

LEFT AND OVERLEAF A GLOSSY-LEAVED CALAMONDIN (*X CITROFORTUNELLA MICRO-CARPA*) AND PELARGONIUMS FIT IN WELL IN A MEDITERRANEAN-STYLE GARDEN. MOST MEDITERRANEAN PLANTS LIKE VERY WELL-DRAINED SOIL, SO BUY GRIT FROM A GARDEN CENTRE AND ADD IT TO THEIR SOIL.

KEY PLANTS

Lavender, pelargoniums, thyme, sage, rosemary, olive and citrus trees, vines, bay, myrtle, rock roses (*Helianthemum*), sun roses (*Cistus*), *Euphorbia characias*, bougainvilleas and oleanders.

FLOWERS IN THE SHADE

If you want to grow flowers in a shady garden, the following plants will provide them in all but the most dismal gloom:

- Japanese anemones (*Anemone x hybrida*): These are wonderful plants that will tolerate fairly deep shade. They produce single or double, white or pink flowers for several weeks in late summer and autumn. My favourite variety is elegant white 'Honorine Jobert'. Well-named 'Whirlwind' has pretty, windswept-looking, white flowers. Some of the pinks are rather wishy-washy, but 'Hadspen Abundance' has attractive, deep pink flowers. Their leaves die down in winter but they re-emerge in spring.

- Camellias: These are the belles of the shady garden. They are evergreen shrubs with glossy leaves and exquisite flowers in winter and spring. Grow them in acid soil – if you don't have acid soil, use ericaceous compost (potting soil) from your garden centre. Frost and early morning sun can ruin the flowers, so a sheltered basement is perfect for them.

- Hydrangeas: Deciduous shrubs that flower reliably in shade. Try lacecaps (flat clusters of flowers) or mop-heads (rounded clusters of flowers). In deep shade, use the oak-leaved type (*Hydrangea quercifolia*), which has white flowers and large, oak-like leaves that turn a fine colour in autumn.

- Rhododendrons: These produce fabulous flowers in the shade. There are hundreds of varieties in just about every colour, and they have attractive evergreen leaves that provide structure in winter, too. Like camellias, they need to be planted in acid soil.

- Busy lizzies (*Impatiens*): These are among the best flowery options for short-term planting in shade (annuals or plants that are replaced after a season). They thrive in sun or shade and have white, pink, purple, red or orange flowers for months on end.

For other flowery seasonal planting in your basement, try annual begonias (*Begonia semperflorens*), pansies, violas, nemophila, lobelia and tobacco plants (*Nicotiana*), all of which can cope well with some shade.

SPECIAL PLANTS FOR SHELTERED GARDENS

If your basement is not too shady, it might be the perfect sheltered (frost-free) environment for growing exotic, not-so-hardy plants. So be the envy of all your big-garden friends and plant these gems:

- Lemon trees (*Citrus limon*): Small evergreen trees with pale green leaves and fragrant white flowers from spring to summer, followed by lemon fruits. They are frost-tender, although they may survive short spells near to 0 °C (32 °F), so take them indoors if frost threatens.

- Calamondins (*x Citrofortunella microcarpa*): Evergreen bushes bearing white flowers in spring and summer, followed by yellow fruits that turn orange. They can withstand temperatures down to 0 °C (32 °F), but should be taken indoors if frost threatens.

- Japanese mock orange (*Pittosporum tobira*): A shrub with leathery evergreen leaves and headily, orange-blossom scented cream-coloured flowers from spring to early summer. The dwarf version (*P. tobira* 'Nanum') is great for pots or small spaces.

- Paperwhite narcissus (*Narcissus papyraceus*): Pure white, strongly scented mini-daffodils in winter and early spring. They will survive in a frost-free garden or, to enjoy their fabulous scent, take them indoors once the buds have formed.

- Mimosa (*Acacia dealbata*): An evergreen tree with feathery grey-green leaves and spikes of fragrant, fluffy yellow flowers from winter through to spring.

- *Clematis armandii*: This has elegant, dark evergreen leaves and starry flowers with a delectable fragrance in early spring. It doesn't need pruning and prefers a sunny wall.

- Gardenia: An evergreen shrub with shiny leaves and waxy, heavily scented white flowers. Take it indoors when the weather is less predictable.

- Lemon verbena: A shrub with delicious lemon-scented leaves, which can be infused to make a good herb tea.

- Passion flower (*Passiflora*): The blue passion flower (*P. caerulea*) is tough enough for many gardens, but it isn't scented. In a sheltered spot, try the unusual *P.* 'Incense', which has extraordinary fragrant purple flowers.

PAINTING SURFACES

Choose two colours that tone well together and complement your plants, containers and furniture. Here, chalky blue and soft lilac have been used for a Mediterranean feel.

1 Prepare the surface you are going to paint by brushing it thoroughly with a stiff wire brush. Rub away any remaining flaking paint with coarse sandpaper and fill any holes with putty suitable for use outside.

2 Use a large paintbrush to apply two coats of pale blue masonry paint evenly over the walls, leaving it to dry thoroughly between coats.

3 Paint the top two rows of bricks with two coats of lilac masonry paint. The steps leading to the upper level of this garden have also been painted to make them more inviting.

BELOW IDENTICAL POTS OF THE SAME PLANT REPEATED UP A FLIGHT OF STEPS CREATE A STYLISH EFFECT. THESE REVERSE-VARIEGATED SPIDER PLANTS (*CHLOROPHYTUM COMOSUM* 'VARIEGATUM') ARE USUALLY GROWN AS HOUSEPLANTS, BUT CAN BE TAKEN OUTSIDE IN WARM WEATHER.

TRADITIONAL

Give yourself a break from the rigours of modern life by making a garden with an old-world feel. You could design the space in a classical manner, adopting the restrained and elegant style of antiquity. Or, you could opt for a nostalgic or retro look; choose a period, such as Victorian, Edwardian, 1950s or 1970s, and decorate the garden with furniture and accessories from that time. Revel in the fantasy that time has stood still in your outdoor room.

GET THE LOOK

- **Classical**: Columns are a must. If you can't afford the real thing, just paint them on the walls or simulate them using lengths of concrete or clay pipe, which you can paint or distress and even top with elegant capitals. Carved stone (or reproduction stone) furniture, urns, obelisks and sculptures all create the look. Trompe l'oeil paintings and frescoes were popular on the walls of Roman gardens. Keep planting restrained and simple, using lush dark green foliage to offset the pale stone: clipped box, yew and

Mediterranean plants such as oleanders and olives would fit the scene, while roses and lilies could provide flowers and fragrance.

- **Victorian**: The Victorians had a craze for coloured bedding plants. Mass production had set in, so gardens were filled with urns, pots, balustrades and ornate clutter (the more you had, the richer you appeared). Grow bright busy lizzies, marigolds, pelargoniums, fuchsias and begonias in cast-iron or stone urns, or formal, shaped flower beds. Elaborate wirework jardinières and ferns were also all the rage and work well in a basement. Complete the look with antique garden furniture and china for a formal tea.

LEFT A MURAL CAN MAKE A TINY GARDEN FEEL LARGER AND PROVIDE COLOUR IN WINTER WHEN PLANTS HAVE DIED BACK. MANY CREATE A THREE-DIMENSIONAL EFFECT AND ALLEVIATE THE CLAUSTRO-PHOBIC FEEL OF ENCLOSING WALLS.

ABOVE RIGHT CHINESE VIRGINIA CREEPER (*PARTHENOCISSUS HENRYANA*) IS AN EASY-TO-GROW, SHADE-TOLERANT CLIMBER THAT IS SELF-CLINGING AFTER INITIAL HELP. ITS WHITE-VEINED LEAVES TURN A FANTASTIC MAGENTA IN AUTUMN BEFORE THEY DROP.

URBAN FRONT GARDENS

First impressions really do matter, so if all you've got in your front garden is an overgrown hedge, cracked concrete and a collection of bottles for recycling, it's time to think again. Don't miss the opportunity to make your home appear warm and welcoming (or dazzlingly elegant). Of course, lack of privacy and security may mean that you don't want to eat (or sunbathe) in your front garden but, with a bit of thought, it could still be a pleasure to come home to. First of all, make the front door accessible. Groping through darkness, tripping over uneven paving and getting your legs lacerated by thorny shrubs is not the best way to come home. Good lighting can provide an effusive welcome and will deter burglars; make sure the paths and steps are lit clearly but subtly, and illuminate the front door with a warm glow.

LOW-EFFORT GARDENING

If you don't want to spend much time in your front garden, create a place that will look good all year round with the minimum of effort. You can have a beautiful garden room to enjoy from indoors, or when you are just passing through, without constant labour.

Flooring

For a low-maintenance space, pave most of the ground in stone slabs, concrete, brick, gravel, cobblestones or crushed stone (a paved surface is the easiest to look after; plants are more time-consuming and a lawn is hard work). If you are using loose stone, make sure you lay it over a geo-textile membrane (which is porous to water but stops weeds coming up), and don't lay it too thickly so that it's easy to walk across. A paved garden needn't look dull: you could use different materials laid in patterns. If the area won't be used or walked on, have some fun with adventurous mixes – why not try a chequerboard of solid stone and crushed slate, or pale and dark cobblestones laid in concentric circles?

Boundaries

When dividing off your garden from the street, consider carefully whether or not you want a hedge. A hedge provides a pleasant leafy greenness (a good antidote to city pavements) and can give a high degree of privacy. The disadvantages are the work (watering, feeding, clipping and clearing up dead leaves) and possible loss of light (particularly in the basement). If you want a hedge, choose a slow-growing type that only needs an annual trim (avoid fast-growing privet; see hedging plants, pages 144–5). Do you really need privacy? If your front garden isn't intended to be a living space, it may be better to keep the space open and easily visible. Railings are easy to maintain and come in a wide range of designs and colours. Alternatively, a solid or picket wooden fence could provide a reasonably inexpensive and low-maintenance barrier.

The Façade

Climbers can be used to completely transform the front of a building. Disguise an ugly façade with vigorous climbers, or train some of the more elegant varieties along balconies and over porches. For an easy life, use self-clinging varieties that don't need tying up, or slow-growing, delicate types that don't need pruning or cutting back (see easy climbers, page 142). Wisteria looks magnificent, but grows wildly and will easily twine up several storeys (see page 70).

LEFT TALL, GALVANIZED STEEL PLANTERS CONTAINING DWARF VARIEGATED BAMBOO (*PLEIOBLASTUS VARIEGATUS*) MAKE A STYLISH ADDITION TO A FRONT DOORSTEP. LOW-GROWING PLANTS COMPLEMENT THE OUTSIZED CONTAINERS. AND HERE, USING ONE TYPE OF PLANT IS MORE EFFECTIVE THAN COMBINING DIFFERENT VARIETIES.

LEFT A RUSTING CROWN MAKES A WITTY ADDITION TO A NEATLY CLIPPED TOPIARY BOX PLANT (*BUXUS SEMPERVIRENS*).
RIGHT SPIKY PURPLE NEW ZEALAND CABBAGE PALMS (*CORDYLINE AUSTRALIS* 'PURPLE TOWER') ADD DRAMA TO A GEOMETRIC FRONT GARDEN.

BELOW RIGHT TRY UNUSUAL MIXTURES OF PLANTS – HERE, GRASSY BLACK LILYTURF (*OPHIOPOGON PLANISCAPUS* 'NIGRESCENS') IS COMBINED WITH A JAPANESE SPINDLE (*EUONYMUS JAPONICUS* 'OVATUS AUREUS') AND A SUCCULENT *ECHEVERIA*, WHICH MUST BE TAKEN INDOORS IN COLD WEATHER.

Planting

For low-effort plants, opt for easy evergreens that need little pruning, provide year-round structure and won't drop all their leaves in autumn (see shade-tolerant evergreens, page 85; for sunny front gardens, see super spiky plants, page 35, and silver and blue plants, page 64). Spreading a 'mulch' of gravel, crushed stone or cobblestones around your plants keeps the soil moist (so it requires less watering), prevents weeds from growing and looks good.

TOPIARY

Using topiary (clipped or trained plants) is an easy way to make an outdoor space look good. Once established (and you can buy ready-made or trained topiary plants), it is fairly effortless and just requires a quick trim a few times in the summer. The distinctive shapes add definition and interest – try a row of pyramids rising out of cobblestones. Use simple, geometric shapes for dramatic impact (and minimum labour) and try repeating the same shape for a superbly stylish effect. To make clipping the shapes easier, use a mould or frame (just place it over the top of the plant and trim).

PARTERRES AND KNOT GARDENS

This is simply a pattern on the ground that is made up of small hedges (in a knot garden the hedges are planted and clipped to look as though they are tied in knots). You can use a single variety of hedge or combine different colours. Try green dwarf box (*Buxus sempervirens* 'Suffruticosa'), silver dwarf lavender (*Lavandula angustifolia* 'Hidcote') and cotton lavender (*Santolina chamaecyparissus*), and purple dwarf barberry (*Berberis thunbergii* 'Atropurpurea Nana'). Knot gardens and parterres look great when viewed from above – try one if your front door is up a flight of steps.

SUITABLE PLANTS FOR TOPIARY

The following can all be clipped to produce topiary shapes:

- Box (*Buxus sempervirens*): This is versatile and can be trimmed to form virtually any shape, from spirals to chickens.

- Yew (*Taxus baccata*): This is also versatile and good for larger shapes. Try monumental obelisks or strutting peacocks.

- Shrubby honeysuckle (*Lonicera nitida*): Fairly fast-growing, so a good choice for impatient gardeners who want fast results, but it needs regular trimming. The tiny leaves allow very precise shapes to be achieved. The gold-leafed variety ('Baggesen's Gold') can also be used.

- Privet (*Ligustrum*): Very fast-growing, so it needs regular trimming, but you won't have to wait years to see results. If you're really enthusiastic, you could plant a privet hedge and turn it into a train (but be prepared to cut it every couple of weeks in summer).

Other possibilities include bay, holly, myrtle, phillyrea and Italian buckthorn.

WINTER AND SPRING FRAGRANT PLANTS

Fill the air with the heady scent of the following perfumers:

- Chinese witch hazel (*Hamamelis mollis*): This has very fragrant, golden-yellow flowers on bare winter branches.
- Wild jonquils (*Narcissus jonquilla*): Produce bright yellow mini-daffodils with an intense fragrance in late spring.
- Violets (*Viola odorata*): These have sweetly scented purple or white flowers in late winter and early spring.
- *Clematis armandii*: An evergreen climber that produces highly fragrant starry white flowers in early spring.
- *Daphne odora*: A small evergreen shrub with fabulously scented winter flowers.
- *Mahonia japonica*: A tough, spiky shrub with yellowish flowers throughout the winter. The flowers smell like lily of the valley.
- Christmas box (*Sarcococca*): A bushy, evergreen shrub with inconspicuous but powerfully fragrant winter flowers.

Other plants to look for include lily of the valley, *Viburnum* 'Anne Russell' and hyacinths, which can be grown indoors or out.

BY THE DOOR

Install a container or two on the doorstep, in the porch or even on the pavement. Using a pair of containers to flank the front door gives it a feeling of importance, but it's essential to keep the plants looking healthy. Choose resilient, easy-to-maintain types if you are likely to forget to water them (see super-tolerant plants for containers, page 104). Permanent evergreens are the easiest choice – just keep them watered and fed – while short-term plants are an option for more enthusiastic gardeners. Go for large, heavy containers (a reclaimed oil drum or a concrete trough) if they could be stolen, or use cheap and cheerful plastic pots of colourful annuals.

FRAGRANT PLANTS

Some of the most deliciously scented plants flower in seasons when the weather is (usually) awful. Don't grow them in the back garden (where you probably won't appreciate them), plant them by the front door and along the path where you'll brush past them even in the depths of winter (see winter and spring fragrant plants, above).

WINDOW LEDGES

Don't let high-rise living put a stop to your horticultural urges. A window ledge is a great place to indulge in a spot of gardening and your efforts will be well appreciated (it's difficult not to notice a window box, particularly if you've gone for something unusual or dramatic). And, of course, the scale makes the task delightfully manageable. If you haven't got wide window ledges, don't worry. Window boxes can be secured on or underneath narrow window sills, or on top of railings and walls. Ask your local garden centre for brackets to hold a box under a ledge. On a narrow sill, put railings around your box to keep it in place. Whatever you do, make sure your containers are firmly secured!

THE CONTAINERS

What size and shape will you use? Choose between made-to-measure boxes, off-the-shelf troughs and a row of smaller containers.

Made-to-measure

Custom-made containers look stylish and streamlined (there's no awkward bit of ledge left over) and they provide maximum plant space. In addition, the bigger the box, the less quickly the soil will dry out. Find a carpenter to make you a container in marine plywood, hardwood or treated softwood. If the wood is attractive, varnish it or treat it with linseed oil; otherwise, paint or stain it. Alternatively, source a custom-made metal container in galvanized steel or zinc from an air-conditioning ducting supplier. Both metals are weatherproof and long-lasting, and can also be painted or enamelled.

Off-the-shelf

Easy, ready-made window boxes are usually plastic, terracotta, wood or reconstituted stone. You may also find galvanized steel and fibreglass troughs. Standard boxes are cheap, but can look mass produced and unexciting. They are often too small to fill up a sill (although you could try to squeeze on two) and generally don't look as sleek as custom-made versions. More unusual troughs in antique stone, copper or lead won't be cheap, but may be beautiful.

Rows of Pots

These can look very chic, but you'll have to be extremely assiduous with the watering can, as little pots dry out fast. If you won't be able to water them daily in warm weather, choose drought-tolerant plants. Try a row of identical pots containing identical plants, or use a mix of the same pot in different colours. A jumble of containers in various shapes, sizes, colours and materials looks good if chosen cleverly.

DECORATING CONTAINERS

With imagination, cheap plastic, wood and terracotta pots and boxes can be vastly improved. Painting is the easiest option; use a single colour or experiment with stripes, checks and spots (see page 73). For a rustic look, paint just the upper half of a terracotta pot and leave the bottom half plain. Use sample pots of paint if you only need a small quantity. Opt for paint effects that work with the plants – a black-and-white zebra pattern would look hip on a trough containing magenta gladioli, while a distressed ochre pot would provide a gentle foil for lavender or rosemary. Apply exterior-grade varnish over the finished design for protection. You could also glue shells, feathers, pebbles, beads, mosaic tiles, fabric, photographs, newspaper or pressed leaves to your containers. Again, apply varnish for a longer-lasting result. Coils of wire, chain, string

LEFT A WINDOW BOX JAM-PACKED WITH PETUNIAS, PELARGONIUMS, LOBELIAS, FUCHSIAS AND HELICHRYSUM WILL PROVIDE A LUXURIANT RIOT OF COLOUR FROM JUNE UNTIL THE FIRST FROST. THE PERMANENT PLANTING OF EVERGREENS IN THE BACKGROUND WILL COME INTO THEIR OWN WHEN THE FLOWERS ARE OVER.

LEFT A GALVANIZED STEEL BOX FOR COLLECTING ASHES FROM A GRATE MAKES AN USUAL CONTAINER FOR THE BIZARRE UPRIGHT IVY (*HEDERA HELIX* 'ERECTA').

BELOW LEFT THIS MODERN TROUGH CONTAINS A PERMANENT PLANTING OF KOHUHU (*PITTOSPORUM TENUIFOLIUM* 'SILVER QUEEN') AND BLACK LILYTURF (*OPHIOPOGON PLANISCAPUS* 'NIGRESCENS').

RIGHT A RECLAIMED COPPER POT SETS OFF A LIME GREEN FERN, EVERGREEN PYGMY BAMBOO (*PLEIOBLASTUS PYGMAEUS*) AND TOBACCO PLANTS (*NICOTIANA SYLVESTRIS*).

BELOW RIGHT A FIERCE CENTURY PLANT (*AGAVE AMERICANA*) IS SURROUNDED BY BLACK LILYTURF AND FLANKED BY GRASSY BLUE FESCUE (*FESTUCA GLAUCA* 'BLAUFUCHS') AND *EUPHORBIA MYRSINITES*.

or rope can be wound around pots as decoration. When deciding on your design, consider the distance from which the container will be viewed. If it will be on an upper floor and barely visible from inside, go for something bold that will be discernible from ground level.

THE PLANTS

Decide whether you want permanent plants (you'll simply need to water, feed and prune them) or whether you want to replant the containers twice a year for seasonal variety. Permanent is less work, but you may want a change (and enjoy the potting). You could use a mixture of some permanent plants with seasonal plants in between. (This is cheaper since you don't need so many new plants.) Tall, airy plants can provide privacy without cutting out too much light (and are far more chic than net curtains!). For maximum daylight indoors during the winter, use plants that are deciduous and drop their leaves. If you know you'll be hopeless at looking after your plants, see super-tolerant plants for containers, page 104.

A window ledge is a great place to grow fragrant plants (see summer scented plants, page 42, and winter and spring fragrant plants, page 98). Leave the window open to let the smell drift inside. Try a row of dwarf lavenders (*Lavandula angustifolia* 'Hidcote'), trailing sweet peas (*Lathyrus odoratus*), or a mix of violets and lily of the valley.

Kitchen window sills cry out for edible plants (see edible flowers, page 146, and easy herbs, pages 152–3). On sunny window ledges, install pots of thyme, rosemary, marjoram and basil. Keep pinching off the tips of the shoots and the plants will stay neat and bushy.

UNUSUAL WINDOW BOXES

For a novel look, try the following permanent plants:

- In a large trough, grow one or two dwarf Japanese maples (*Acer palmatum*). These mini-trees drop their pretty leaves in autumn to reveal an elegant tracery (so sunlight won't be excluded). Choose a tiny, slow-growing variety like 'Garnet', 'Red Pygmy' or 'Corallinum'. Grow them on a sheltered ledge and keep the soil moist.
- For a dramatic, spiky look, plant a row of evergreen New Zealand flax. Use the dwarf type called 'Bronze Baby'. Its strappy leaves will grow up to 60–80 cm (24–32 in) tall and provide you with some privacy.
- On a sheltered, sunny ledge, the honey bush (*Melianthus major*) should be evergreen. If it gets too cold, it will die back to ground level over winter, but it will grow back again in spring. It has large ferociously toothed, blue-green leaves. Cut it back in spring if it gets too big.
- On a cool, shady ledge, ever-green ferns are perfect. Enjoy the spectacle of the new fronds unfurling. Try the soft shield fern (*Polystichum setiferum* Divisilobum group), the sword fern (*Polystichum munitum*) or the Japanese tassel fern (*Polystichum polyblepharum*).
- Grasses look fantastic on a window ledge. For a minimalist feel, plant just one type. Try small blue fescue (*Festuca glauca* 'Blaufuchs'), yellow-striped Bowles' golden sedge (*Carex hachijoensis* 'Evergold') or larger, orange pheasant's tail grass (*Stipa arundinacea*). All of these are evergreen.
- A dwarf evergreen bamboo is chic. Hunt for pygmy bamboo (*Pleioblastus pygmaeus*), which reaches 40 cm (16 in) high. If you have a tall window and want to create a screen, use *Pleioblastus auricomus*, which has terrific, brilliant yellow- and green-striped leaves, gets to 1.5 m (5 ft) high and grows in sun or part shade. However, don't put bamboos on a windy ledge and keep their soil moist.
- A row of century plants (*Agave americana*), with their spine-tipped, rigid, serrated leaves, look undeniably exotic. Grow them on a sheltered, sunny ledge. The plain green type is the toughest, while the striped varieties probably won't survive a frost. They are drought tolerant.

SUPER-TOLERANT PLANTS FOR CONTAINERS

These uncomplaining stalwarts should survive despite the most appalling neglect (but water and feed them when you remember). They are all evergreen.

- Spindle (*Euonymus fortunei*): A sprawling, bushy plant. 'Silver Queen' has white-splashed dark green leaves that become pink-tinged in winter. 'Emerald 'n' Gold' has bright green and yellow leaves. Suitable for sun or shade and drought tolerant.

- Periwinkle (*Vinca minor* or *major*): This has dark green leaves that grow along trailing stems. Purple, violet, blue or white flowers appear intermittently from spring to autumn. Some have cream- or yellow-patterned leaves. Compact 'Gertrude Jekyll' has white flowers and 'Atropurpurea' has dark plum-purple flowers. It is drought tolerant and suitable for sun or shade, but flowers better in sun.

- Ivy (*Hedera*): Super-tolerant; some are very pretty. Check out tiny green 'Duckfoot' (the leaves are shaped like webbed feet), bright yellow 'Buttercup', silvery grey-splashed 'Glacier', yellow-speckled 'Luzii' and

weird upright 'Erecta'. Suitable for growing in sun or shade and drought tolerant.

- Mrs Robb's bonnet (*Euphorbia amygdaloides* var. *robbiae*): This has whorls of leathery, dark green leaves on upright stems. Clusters of long-lasting lime-green flowers appear in spring and summer. Suitable for sun or shade and drought tolerant.

- Thyme, lavender and rosemary: All hate being overwatered, so suit anyone who frequently forgets. They like lots of sun. Avoid growing them in a place where their soil will be soggy during the rainy months.

- Lilyturf (*Liriope muscari*): This has strappy green leaves and funky spikes of purple flowers in autumn. It requires shade and tolerates erratic watering.

- *Pachysandra terminalis*: This makes a lush carpet of dark green leaves about 20 cm (8 in) high. There is a type with white-margined leaves, too. It is drought tolerant and best grown in shade.

Other resilient plants include stinking hellebore (*Helleborus foetidus*), the houseleeks (*Sempervivums*), the male fern (*Dryopteris filix-mas*), which is not evergreen, and the castor oil plant (*Fatsia japonica*).

On shady window ledges, opt for mint. You could grow various different types, including peppermint, apple mint, pineapple mint, ginger mint and even eau de Cologne mint.

Permanent Plants

For an easy life, grow permanent plantings of evergreens. In shade, you could grow *Skimmia japonica* 'Rubella', which is a tolerant, compact bush with decorative clusters of tiny red buds that last through autumn and winter. (Replace it if it gets too big and leggy). The Corsican hellebore (*Helleborus argutifolius*) can be grown in sun or shade and has handsome, dark green leaves and exotic-looking pale green flowers. On a sunny ledge, try aromatic cotton lavender (*Santolina chamaecyparissus*), which has yellow pompom flowers in summer. To keep it compact and tidy, clip it after flowering. For a modern look, grow drought-tolerant black lilyturf (*Ophiopogon planiscapus* 'Nigrescens'), which has strappy blackish leaves that contrast well with silvery foliage. Box (*Buxus sempervirens*) is an excellent window-ledge plant that can be clipped to form architectural shapes. It is usually plain green but there are variegated types, too – 'Elegantissima' has white-margined leaves. Keep it reasonably well watered or it will turn brown and die.

Seasonal Planting

Plant summer bedding plants in spring, but keep them indoors until all risk of frost has passed, or wrap them up if frost threatens (use newspaper, cardboard or horticultural fleece). There's a huge range that will flower through the summer and into autumn (particularly if you deadhead them, see page 46). Some of the best and most long-flowering are the marguerites (margaritas) (*Argyranthemum*). The usual type has white flowers with a yellow centre; for a change, grow 'Vancouver' (starry pink flowers) or 'Jamaica Primrose' (warm yellow flowers). Deadhead them regularly, don't overwater them and grow them in well-drained soil. Easy, drought-tolerant pelargoniums also flower for months (many flower all year if it's warm enough). Some have scented foliage, some have trailing stems and some have multi-coloured leaves. They prefer (and flower better in) sun, but will cope with some shade. Helichrysum is invaluable for mixed plantings. It has lovely felty leaves on trailing stems, which mingle with other

LEFT STIFFLY SPIKY CENTURY PLANTS (*AGAVE AMERICANA*) IN WIRE BASKETS ARE ATTACHED TO THE WALL BENEATH A LENGTH OF ANTIQUE INDIAN FRETWORK, MAKING AN ECLECTIC AND IMAGINATIVE ADORNMENT UNDER A WINDOW.

plants and help tie a display together. Choose between lime green, silvery grey, variegated or a miniature version with tiny silvery grey leaves. Other easy-to-grow summer flowers include pot marigolds (*Calendula officinalis*), annual lobelia (*Lobelia erinus cultivars*), bidens, gazanias, nasturtiums, Swan River daisies (*Brachycome*), diascias, busy lizzies (*Impatiens*), fuchsias, Livingstone daisies (*Mesembryanthemum*), tobacco plants (*Nicotiana*), petunias and African marigolds (*Tagetes*).

In autumn, fill containers with fresh plants that will look good all through winter and spring. Perennial (longer-lived) foliage plants can be used to bulk up plantings. Once the display is over, transplant them. Use thyme (including golden and silver variegated forms), small ivies, small hebes, *Eunoymus fortunei*, bugle or checkerberry (*Gaultheria procumbens*). And don't forget to plant spring bulbs underneath your winter display for a bit of vernal excitement.

There are far fewer container plants that provide winter flowers. One of the best options is heather (*Erica carnea*). These bushy evergreen plants have needle-like leaves and tiny flowers in colours ranging from white to red from mid-winter to spring. They must be grown in acid soil, so use ericaceous compost (potting soil). Bellis daisies (*Bellis perennis* Pomponette Series) bear fluffy pink and white daisies, while winter-flowering violas and pansies (the Ultima, Universal and Universal Plus series are excellent) also produce flowers throughout winter and spring (except in severe weather), but deadhead them regularly. Some primulas, polyanthus and primroses also flower in winter, and they come in a wide choice of colours. For autumn flowers, include cyclamen (*Cyclamen hederifolium*), which have beautiful silver-marbled, dark green leaves that last through winter and die back in early summer. They are perennial and come up year after year. Other (very different) winter foliage plants are the ornamental cabbages. They may not appeal to everyone, but these mock vegetables are certainly colourful. The colours get more intense as temperatures fall, but they begin to fade after mid-winter.

CONTAINER PLANTING

First water the plant well. Put a layer of drainage material, 3 cm (1¼ in) or more deep, into the bottom of the container – use leica, broken terracotta, gravel, stones or polystyrene (styrofoam) chunks. Remove the plant from its pot and plant it in fresh compost (potting soil) in its new container. Keep the plant at the same level as it was in its original pot; try to make this about 2 cm (¾ in) below the rim. Firm the plant into its new home by patting the compost down around it and then water it thoroughly.

CHEAT'S WINDOW BOX

Instead of planting seasonal flowers in soil in your window box, just put them straight into the box in their individual plastic pots. This is not a permanent solution, but it means you can easily replace the plants when they begin to look tired (or when you feel like a change). Put a layer of water-retaining clay granules into the base of the window box to help keep the compost or soil in the plastic pots moist. Feed and water the plants as normal, but remember that small pots can dry out quickly.

the elements

The range of materials that can be used successfully in a contemporary garden is exciting, and adventurous tastes can really be indulged. Today's urban gardens have no link with the natural landscape, so there is little constraint as to what looks out of place. Also, modern gardens are often small, so more expensive and time-consuming options like mosaic flooring are feasible. Designs and themes can be harvested from around the world. It's more important that the garden ties in with the interior decor and surrounding architecture than follows a prescribed garden style. Of course, in some gardens, traditional materials work best, echoing the building and complementing the interior design, while in others, organic materials can provide relief from the built environment. From rubber floors to bamboo screens, once you have decided on a style, there's a wealth of possibilities for creating the perfect look. Keep the design and choice of materials simple and uncluttered – too much squeezed into a small garden could turn it into a junk shop. And don't forget the practicalities: maintenance, life-span, cost and ease of use will all impact on the success of your outdoor room. The sections below set out some of the options, – check them out for inspiration and ideas.

FLOORING

The choice of flooring for a garden is very important. It makes an enormous visual and psychological impact and can dramatically affect the way an outdoor space will be used. There is a world of difference in both atmosphere and function between a garden with a lawn covering the main area, one paved with concrete slabs and one spread with gravel. Choose the type of flooring that allows you to use the space as you want and that creates the style you have decided on for your outdoor room.

What do you want to do in your garden? Paved areas are great for heavy, frequent and year-round use, for placing furniture on, for dining out, for children (unless they fall over), for parties and dancing. Lawns are good for lounging, exercising, picnics and doing cartwheels. If you want to pad around with bare feet, think about the sensation underfoot. Make sure the flooring will work in your space: some floors get slippery in shade, while others get uncomfortably hot in direct sun. Consider maintenance and wear and tear: forget the fragile camomile lawn if you're a family of soccer addicts.

Flooring is often the most expensive element in the garden, so make sure you get it right. Who wants to shovel sacks and sacks of chipped stone back into bags because you've decided it looks like a giant outdoor litter tray and the local cats think so too? Of course, if it's easy to change, you could install temporary flooring for fun – perhaps a lawn on your balcony? Or a few bags of sand for a beach on your roof?

mixing and matching

Outdoors, uncomplicated flooring usually looks best. Plants provide wonderful shapes and textures and are best set against a simple floor. But if the plants and ornaments are kept simple, the paving can become more adventurous. If you are paving a large area, using two different materials (like brick and stone), laid in an attractive pattern, visually breaks up the area and prevents it from looking like a highway.

grass

A well-kept lawn is a delight to behold. It can provide a wonderfully calm, comfortable pool of green, but in the wrong conditions (or if it's not looked after properly), it will become a scruffy mud patch.

Grass can also be allowed to grow long and be cut just once in late summer and once in the autumn for a wild-flower meadow effect. Plant bulbs and naturalistic flowers in the grass. In small areas of meadow, dwarf bulbs look best: use snowdrops, crocuses and dwarf daffodils like 'February Gold' and 'Jenny', and don't mow the lawn until most of the foliage has died down.

PROS AND CONS
- *Grass is cheap.*
- *It's a soft surface for young children to play on.*
- *If you want a lawn, you'll need somewhere to store a mower (unless you hire someone who brings their own).*
- *A lawn doesn't work well in a shady or well-used space.*
- *Unless you particularly enjoy regular and repetitive tasks, a lawn is a bore to look after.*

concrete

Concrete isn't always lumpy and grey; it can be cast in situ for wonderful smooth expanses and customized shapes. And not only that, in-situ concrete can be treated to produce a range of finishes. Power-blasted when almost dry, the pebbles and gravel in it become exposed, creating a rugged texture. It can also be polished, carved, brushed or dyed. But if you still don't like the look of it, you can paint it with masonry paint.

Concrete also comes in a huge choice of precast units – bricks, hexagons, squares, random rectangles and circles, not to mention fake-log slices! And some concrete reproduction stone is very convincing and is far cheaper than the real thing.

PROS AND CONS
- *Concrete can be extremely cheap and a good alternative to natural stone.*
- *It is very flexible – think of a shape: you can probably achieve it with concrete.*
- *Precast concrete units vary widely in quality and attractiveness. Some are great, some are foul.*

- *It is low maintenance and usually long-lasting.*
- *Non-slip finishes are good for shady gardens.*

natural stone slabs

If you've got the money, this is a wonderful choice. For a softer look, fill the gaps between the slabs with soil instead of mortar to allow plants to grow in them. Random rectangular shapes look good with traditional architecture, while the graphic effect of perfect squares may work better with modern buildings. With crazy paving, proceed with care!

PROS AND CONS
- *Natural stone is very versatile: you can buy a type of stone to suit almost any style of architecture. The options include slate, granite, marble and sandstone. Sizes vary from tiny mosaic tiles through small blocks called setts to enormous slabs; while finishes range from rough chiselled to highly polished.*
- *It can be eye-wateringly expensive.*
- *Stone can look terrible if it's badly laid, so pay someone to do it properly.*
- *It's long-lasting and durable,*

and most types of stone get better with age.
- *Although stone is easy to maintain, weeding between the slabs and hosing down may be necessary.*
- *Some types of stone get slippery in the shade or when wet, while others become hot in direct sun.*

bricks and pavers

Bricks are great for making paths, steps and small seating areas, or for edging and making patterns in other paving. Large expanses of brick can look too busy, though. For a coherent effect, choose bricks that match those in surrounding architecture, and always use frostproof bricks outside or they will flake apart. Bricks needn't be red: look for slate-coloured engineering bricks or yellowish-brown stock bricks.

PROS AND CONS
- *Although they are quite expensive to buy and lay, bricks are affordable when used over a small area.*
- *Bricks are available in a wide range of colours, finishes and shapes. Smooth new bricks look surprisingly modern, while reclaimed bricks give a ready-aged effect.*

be laid loose (but don't lay it too thickly over areas you will walk across or it will be like wading through porridge) or, for a firmer surface, a top dressing of gravel can be rolled into hoggin (a mixture of gravel and clay).

A high-tech option is to resin-bond gravel or sand in place to create an immovable, textured surface. If you're feeling adventurous, you could create geometric or swirling patterns of multicoloured gravel or sand and get them secured in place on the ground with resin.

Crushed stone is an attractive alternative to gravel, and colours range from white to black. Modern and quirky alternatives to gravel include artificially coloured chippings (you could spray-paint your own in silver or gold), crushed glass (this comes in a kaleidoscope of colours, some of which look very artificial), metal washers, bottle tops and seashells.

PROS AND CONS

- *Gravel and crushed stone is available in a wide range of colours and sizes. Use large sizes if there are cats about*

- *Bricks can be laid in various patterns including herring-bone, basketweave (as shown above) and stretcher bond.*

cobblestones and pebbles

These wonderful, water-worn stones can be set in mortar to form paths and small areas of paving, or used loose over terraces and around plants. When you set them in mortar, make sure they are laid as tightly together as possible so you can't see too much of the mortar. Get creative and lay them in beautiful patterns using different colours and sizes. If you're laying stones loose, do so over a geo-textile membrane to stop weeds growing up between them. Loose cobblestones or pebbles are also useful as an easily removable covering for a manhole cover that needs to be kept accessible.

gravel and crushed stone

An extremely versatile option, gravel can be used for paths, driveways and sitting areas, and it looks great spread between plants. It can either

and try a sample in the garden first to make sure the colour looks right.

- It's generally an inexpensive option and usually much cheaper than solid stone.
- Loose stone laid near the house may become irritating because it can be brought in on the soles of shoes.
- It's easy to lay; you can do it yourself.
- Gravel or crushed stone can be laborious to weed, so lay it over a geo-textile membrane (which can be found in most garden centres) to stop weeds growing up through it.
- It's not very comfortable to walk on with bare feet: some types are agonizing.

clay tiles

From plain to patterned and glazed, there are masses of different types of tiles. Mellow terracotta tiles are redolent of sunny climes and provide a pleasant warm atmosphere. Glazed tiles can look gaudy in the natural landscape but are great in a small urban space. Check that they have a non-slip finish if you intend to walk on them. Roofing tiles can be laid on edge (with just a thin slice visible) as a decorative element within other paving. Make sure that any tiles you use in your garden are frostproof and can be used outside.

decking

Brilliant for use on roof terraces that get the benefit of full sun, decking has a wonderful relaxed feel and evokes memories of jetties and beach huts. It comes in a range of wood, from iroko to pine. (If you choose a hardwood, check that it definitely comes from a renewable source.) Decking can be varnished, stained or painted, and a good selection of coloured wood stains is now available. Apply a UV protector every year or two if you don't want your deck to fade or weather to a silvery colour.

Before you begin laying it out, decide how you want to arrange your boards: don't leave it to chance because this can make a big difference visually. Boards laid across a narrow space make it seem wider, while boards laid lengthways make it appear longer (avoid this in a narrow town garden). You can also buy squares of decking that can be slotted together for an instant floor. They may not fit your space perfectly, but you can use them as a quick solution to hide ugly paving or an unattractive flat roof.

PROS AND CONS

- Decking is not a cheap option. Well-laid hardwood decking comes at a hefty price, but it doesn't rot. Softwood decking is cheaper, but needs regular painting with preservative.
- It can get hazardously slippery, particularly in damp and shady spots. (In this case, ribbed decking is better.)
- Decking is not totally low maintenance – preservatives must be applied to keep it in good condition, and algae needs to be scrubbed off to prevent it from becoming like an ice rink. Ribbed decking traps dirt and leaves, so it needs regular sweeping.
- It's good for sloping sites: decks can form a series of terraces without the need for major earthworks.
- Seats, tables, plant boxes and sandboxes can all be easily made in the same wood and incorporated into the design.
- Good-quality decking is lovely underfoot, but beware of splinters in cheaper wood.

railway sleepers

These have a wonderful industrial feel and can give weight and structure to an outside space. Select them yourself from reclaimed timber yards: some are full of oil, and in hot weather they will ooze and make a horrible mess. They make great steps and edgings for raised beds, but don't sit on them unless you're in your overalls.

logs and wood chippings

These look good in a wild or woodland garden. Sawn into slices, logs can be used to make a stepping-stone path through plants. Laid on their sides, whole logs can form a rustic path (but only for those who are nimble on their feet). For a cheap path, use wood chips with wooden edging to help contain the chippings. This is not a neat option, since birds tend to spread the chips around.

sand and grit

Sand comes in a wide range of colours, although golden yellow is easiest to get hold of. Avoid using builder's sand in your garden as it can stain. Little children will enjoy playing in their own sandpit, and sitting with your feet in sand is a delicious sensation – try making a recessed box full of sand underneath your outdoor dining table! Cover it whenever you are not using it to keep pets and rain out. Grit can be raked into sensual swirls and looks good in Japanese-style gardens.

rubber and plastic

Synthetic rubber or plastic floors are a great option in contemporary urban gardens. Choose a funky colour and trim it to fit your mini Eden. Alternatively, look for rubber or plastic tiles. Comfortable underfoot, easy to lay and to wash down, good if you have small children, and fairly cheap – what more could you want? After all, linoleum is widely used indoors.

astroturf

Plastic grass gives the impression of greenery, and you don't have to mow it. Astroturf is light, so it works well on roof terraces. For a different effect, try it in brown

or black. It's very easy to lay, as it can simply be rolled out and cut to fit; no sticking down is necessary. For a visual link, why not have a plastic-grass rug indoors, too?

metal

Metal grilles make great stairs, walkways and balconies. They have an airy feel, won't cut out too much light and allow a view through, perhaps to planting or the street far below. On a grille balcony, you can almost feel as if you're floating in space. This surface is not comfortable for walking on barefoot, though.

Sheet metal can make an interesting modern floor. Corten gives a fantastic industrial effect. It's a type of steel that rusts to a warm orange colour, then self-seals so it doesn't deteriorate further. The resulting rusted surface is not too slippery.

glass

Don't overlook glass for flooring. Laid on its own or in panels flush with other flooring, it is very useful for allowing light into a room below, and thick glass can be walked over. Use sandblasted glass if you don't want to see through it.

mosaic

Customize your floor with a mosaic. The sky's the limit when you're choosing what to use. Play around with recycled and found objects like broken dishes, tiles, wine-bottle bases, metal cogs, fossils, pebbles, glass beads, marbles and shells. Site the mosaic somewhere subtle if you are worried that the design may become tiresome if it's seen too often. You could lift up a paving slab and lay your mosaic in a soft concrete mix. If it goes horribly wrong, you can always put the slab back.

TEMPORARY SURFACES

Don't forget about the design possibilities offered by temporary flooring. Raffia, rattan, reed, and split bamboo matting is inexpensive, easy to roll out and great for hiding unattractive paving and scruffy grass. It should last for at least a summer and can then be replaced. On dry days, spread out indoor blankets and picnic rugs in the garden. Plastic mats can look colourful and will protect floor cushions (just throw them out when they become tatty).

BOUNDARIES & SCREENS

The way in which garden boundaries are built makes a big impact on the atmosphere within and requires careful thought. First, work out what your particular boundaries need to achieve. Should they give a sense of enclosure and protection? Delimit a space without obscuring a view or cutting out light? Keep people out (or children or animals in)? Give shelter from wind or block out noise? Try to resist the temptation to automatically opt for maximum privacy by putting up a tall and solid divide all around the limits of your plot. In a small space, this can lead to the highly undesirable sensation of being in a cell. And in any case, if your garden is overlooked from above, naked sunbathing would still be hazardous.

Weigh up the pros and cons of a solid boundary. See-through trellis, railings or plants give a greater sense of space and allow light and air to circulate. These options also provide a fair degree of privacy, unless your neighbours really want to look at you (which they probably don't). But solid boundaries may be necessary to screen things from view. Could you combine sections of solid material with sections of see-through? Could you simply put trellis on top of an existing wall or fence for greater privacy?

Grow plants around the boundaries of your garden. Walls and fences give a clear indication of the extent of the garden, but thick planting can blur the boundaries, disguising rather than emphasizing the limits of the space.

If you have inherited a jumble of different types of boundary fence from neighbours on all sides, consider covering these with a single material for a more restful effect. You could also customize boundaries with salvaged or found objects and clever purchases such as bamboo canes nailed in a lattice pattern. If you're building a wall, you could set some mirror tiles into it, or an ancient ammonite (but remember that it may be illegal to remove these from the natural landscape, so buy one from a reputable source). Or, attach contrasting panels to spice up plain walls or fencing: try woven hazel hurdles, or Moorish metal fretwork.

using screens

You can use dividers within your garden to create a series of 'rooms' or distinct areas. These needn't be above eye level: a low wall may be sufficient to create the suggestion of a different space and give variety to the garden.

A garden is far more interesting if the whole thing cannot be taken in at a glance. Looking out at the back fence is not a tantalizing prospect. Hidden areas to explore will create a sense of mystery and draw people out. Even in a small space, screens can be used to create areas that aren't immediately visible – this can also make the garden seem larger. A tall, airy shrub or a section of trellis halfway along the garden could be enough

to obscure what lies behind. Screens are also useful for creating areas out of the public eye. If the garden is overlooked, a seat behind a well-positioned partition can be completely private (and far more enticing).

wooden fences

Natural wood fits in well in a garden, although it can also be painted or stained for far-from-rustic effects. Softwood fences will not last forever and they require regular painting or treatment with preservative. Hardwood fences are more durable, but more expensive.

PANEL AND CLOSEBOARD

For instant privacy, these can be erected to form a visual barrier. A panel fence is made up of large, preconstructed pieces whereas, in a closeboard fence, vertical boards are individually nailed in place to horizontal supports. These fences are often not beautifully finished, but serve well as a background (attach trellis and climbing plants to improve them). Panel fences tend to come in unattractive shades of yellowish brown, but they can be stained (or painted) to look far better. You can also improve the

appearance of a panel fence by attaching finials or caps on top of its posts.

PROS AND CONS

- *Panels provide cheap, off-the-shelf fencing while closeboard is more expensive.*
- *Make sure that your panel fence has been treated with preservative and that it is constructed with rustproof nails or staples. Properly maintained, it should easily last between 10 and 20 years.*
- *Tall, non-transparent fences can feel claustrophobic.*

PICKET FENCES

These charming, usually low, fences are often seen around country cottage gardens. They can also look good along a town front garden. Pointed white picket fences are the classic type; for a less obvious effect, use uprights with rounded or square-cut ends, and paint the fence an unusual colour.

PROS AND CONS

- *For hip stripes, you could paint the uprights in a mixture of colours.*
- *Picket fences are a cheap alternative to costly wrought-iron railings.*

- *While they afford little privacy, they can be used to contain children and animals.*

trellis

Although trelliswork will not give you absolute privacy, it is good for preserving a feeling of space and provides a great surface for climbing plants (see climbers for shady gardens, page 86, and easy climbers, page 142). The size of the holes in the trellis determines how much the garden is screened from view. Trellis is also useful for setting on top of existing walls and fences for extra height and privacy.

Trellis needn't be made from sawn wood: look for willow, hazel or bamboo. Along with classical square and diamond lattice designs, you can also find contemporary vertical or horizontal slatted trellis (with the cross-pieces behind barely visible). Alternatively, make your own by nailing slats to a frame. You could also create a free-standing screen by hinging three narrow trellis panels together. Trellis can be painted or stained to blend (or clash) with nearby plants. Red trellis would look wonderful in contrast with lush green planting.

brick and stone walls

These are marvellous, long-lasting boundaries that can be built to any height. Modern bricks or square-cut stone look contemporary, while rough stone and reclaimed bricks have a traditional or more rustic feel. A brick wall can be built honeycomb-style with holes in it. Think carefully before you paint your walls. Once applied, paint is difficult to remove, and walls may need to be repainted regularly (which can be tricky if you've decided to grow climbers up the wall).

PROS AND CONS
- *Brick and stone walls are expensive, but long-lasting.*
- *In a small space, these heavy, non-transparent structures may be oppressive.*
- *They are generally maintenance-free unless painted, although repointing will eventually be necessary.*
- *Bricks absorb water, so the soil near a wall may get very dry and less easy for plants.*

concrete

Concrete blocks make strong, inexpensive, solid walls. Left unpainted and unrendered, they have a coarse (but appealing), utilitarian look. If you decide to have them rendered (a cement or plaster mortar is applied to the surface), make sure it's done effectively; otherwise, the outlines of the blocks can show through, giving an unattractive, cheap result. A range of finishes can be achieved on rendered walls: try smooth, textured, patterned or – deeply unfashionable – pebble-dashed.

In-situ concrete may be used to create elegant, sculptural walls. These can also be made with various finishes and can be painted or colourwashed. To make the walls, concrete is poured into moulds that are usually made from planks (known as shuttering). Use overlapping, rough-grained wood for the shuttering and the surface of the concrete will be organically textured. Concrete fits in particularly well in contemporary gardens and with modern architecture.

metal railings

Solid, wrought-iron railings are stylish and look great outside traditional buildings. Painted black, perhaps with gold finials, they give an expensively elegant look. Cast iron is cheaper, but it can look mass produced. Plain hollow railings are fairly cheap and can form a pleasant, no-nonsense boundary. Experiment with railings in different metals, finishes and paint colours, and, to put your plot right at the cutting edge, consider investing in modern, custom-made metal railings.

mesh and chain-link

A fantastic choice in many small gardens, these provide excellent support for plants and allow light and air to penetrate, so avoiding a feeling of being boxed in. Although some mesh and chain-link fences can look very utilitarian, they may fit in well in a modern garden. If you choose a dark colour, they become almost invisible when covered in climbers. Avoid high chain-link fences unless you want a tennis-court effect.

Grille or mesh fencing can provide a reasonable degree of privacy, particularly if the mesh is close-knit and it is densely covered in climbing plants. Chain-link fencing is very cheap; mesh is also generally inexpensive.

metal panels

Brushed or polished, smooth sheets of metal can enliven a small space. Use them to create shimmering light and misty reflections. They brighten up shady spots and have a clean, modernist look. Enamel can be applied to metal sheets (like steel) for brilliant hues, and should also make the panels weatherproof.

hedges

These living boundaries increase the amount of greenery in small gardens and provide relief from the surrounding built environment. For a year-round screen, choose an evergreen type. Flowering and scented hedges are delightful, particularly near a terrace or the front door (see hedging plants, pages 144–5).

PROS AND CONS
- *Hedges can be surprisingly expensive if you buy decent-sized plants. Bare-rooted plants are a cheaper option.*
- *These are high-maintenance boundaries. Fast-growing varieties (like privet) require regular trimming, although others, like box, yew and beech, need just an annual haircut. They also require feeding and watering to stay in tip-top condition.*
- *Depending on height and density, hedges afford varying degrees of privacy.*
- *They may take up too much space – a tall hedge is at least 50 cm (20 in) wide.*
- *It can take time for a hedge to reach the desired height.*
- *Hedges are better windbreaks than solid walls or fences.*

glass bricks and panels

Valuable for preserving light, glass can form a strong, modern and stylish boundary. Glass bricks may be used to distort the view into a garden, giving some privacy. Or use sand-blasted glass for good screening. Panes of coloured or stained glass could also be incorporated into a wall.

fabric

Curtains made from strong sailcloth or non-rip nylon are an excellent option if you want to control the weather or view. They work particularly well on a balcony or roof terrace. Attach them to firmly secured metal poles using hoops designed to slide along the poles.

OTHER OPTIONS
- Living willow fences (made from woven willow sticks, which carry on growing when they are pushed into the ground), woven hazel hurdles and reed panels.
- Bamboo: thick, whole canes can be bound together for a rigid non-transparent screen. Panels or rolls of split bamboo should last for about five years outside.
- Polycarbonate sheeting (used on conservatory roofs) makes a stylish modern boundary, and could be used as a windbreak on a small roof terrace.
- For covering a variety of fences, try rolls of dried heather, coppiced willow or peeled reed.
- For a low divider, drill holes in pieces of wood or upright stones to make 'posts' for suspending ropes or chains.
- Rural wooden post-and-rail or single rail fences.
- Plastic netting (it is used by farmers as a windbreak; you could do the same).
- Reproduction wood won't rot and is maintenance-free.
- Use tiles or reclaimed roofing slates to cover plain walls. Just nail them on overlapping from the bottom up.
- Decking can be used to clad walls. For a uniform look, use the same wood on the floor.

gates

A handsome or unusual gate makes a big impression on visitors, so don't unthinkingly install something purely functional. Make sure the gate opens into the garden, so people are drawn in. Metal gates vary from the stark and simple with straight uprights to the flamboyantly curved and patterned. You could grow plants nearby to echo the design (perhaps spiky-leaved irises planted by a gate with a pointed top). Wooden gates could either be picket-style to match adjoining fencing or solid for more privacy. You could consider choosing a more unusual material for your gate: a panel of beaten bronze or copper, a slab of textured glass or a leather curtain might look fantastic.

mirrors

Cleverly used, mirrors can work wonders in a small garden. They create the illusion of greater space and increase the light levels. Shrouded in foliage or surrounded by a false doorway, a mirror can look like an alluring opening through to another garden room. Place a mirror behind a foliage-covered trellis to double the greenery or tilt one skywards to bring down reflections of the sky.

Don't put anything in front of your mirror that will give the game away. The double reflection of a round table and chairs would look ridiculous, but a line of matching pots leading right up to a mirror can simply appear longer, the deception going undetected. Make sure a garden mirror is angled so you can't see yourself in it. Tilt it away from the door leading outside and any other viewpoint, or you may find yourself staring back eerily from the end of the garden.

You could place mirrors on interior walls to reflect the garden and bring it indoors; it's cheaper than buying a beautiful painting, and a changing green tapestry can be enjoyed. A mirror can also be used in conjunction with water. Placed behind a pool, it will double its apparent size. Mirrors can make a stream go on forever or be used to line the bottom of a very shallow pool to make it appear deeper.

OVERHEAD STRUCTURES

In many gardens, overhead structures are not exploited enough. Giving an outdoor room a ceiling is a clever way to create a sense of intimacy or to offset surrounding (often oppressively high) walls and buildings. And of course, some overhead structures provide protection from the elements and privacy from neighbours. The structure needn't be solid: a few wires or metal struts might be sufficient to define the space. Alternatively, moveable overhead structures may be useful and can be pulled across as the rain sets in.

pergolas

Plant-festooned pergolas can be used over a terrace to create a charming living space (and provide delicious dappled shade), or for green, enclosed walkways in the garden. In an overlooked garden, they provide a partial overhead screen, giving a sense of privacy while allowing light and air to penetrate. Wood or metal are traditionally used for pergolas, but choose whatever fits in with your garden style. Polished steel

tubes or copper plumbing pipes may look right, or rustic wooden poles, still covered with the bark, could be used for an entirely different effect. Some pergolas are built with brick or stone pillars for uprights and wooden or metal beams across the top. Narrow strips of trellis can also be used to make the uprights, giving a delicate effect and providing excellent support for climbers.

Grow grapevines, golden hop, wisteria or Virginia creeper over a pergola near the house. They all drop their leaves in autumn so, on winter days, they won't cut out precious light. Scented flowers are a bonus: use roses, jasmine, honeysuckle, some clematis (*Clematis montana* var. *rubens* 'Elizabeth' and evergreen *Clematis armandii* both have a delicious fragrance) or try the less hardy star jasmine (*Trachelospermum jasminoides*).

Instead of growing plants over your pergola, you could stretch fabric curtains between the posts and beams. These could be pulled aside when they are not needed and would also

look great illuminated at night. For a bright, airy feel, use fresh white or cream materials.

arches

An arch gives instant height and impact to a garden. Use one to frame a view, offering (hopefully) tantalizing glimpses of what lies beyond. An arch can also be used to support climbing plants and will serve as an interesting focal point. To make your garden more intriguing, screen an area from view using an arch flanked by tall planting or trellis.

Arches are made in a range of materials, wood or metal being the most common. Metal may look more delicate (and be less dominating in a small space), but it can also be expensive. Paint metal arches black or dark green for a traditional look. Rusting metal might work well in a more modern garden. Wooden arches can be elegantly smooth (try

varnished, stained or painted arches), or unaffectedly natural (those made from untreated bark-covered branches). Arches can also be made from woven willow, hazel, bamboo, brick or stone. An arch needn't be symmetrical: a lopsided creation might look better in an informal garden. Decide whether your arch needs to be kept simple (perhaps a single hoop of metal over a path) or more elaborate.

arbours

An arbour is an intimate place where you can sit and unwind. It generally consists of a seat or bench underneath an overhead structure, which may not be solid (or rainproof). Like arches, arbours are usually made of metal or wood. They work best in a secluded spot, perhaps where you can catch the evening sun. For absolute bliss, surround and smother your arbour with fragrant plants.

awnings

These are incredibly popular with restaurant owners but, strangely, they are under-used in home settings. They can be rolled out to give protection from the sun or rain and have a lovely vacation (or restaurant!) feel. Cheap and easy to construct,

an awning could simply be made from a robust piece of fabric like waterproof canvas or tough polyester, which can be attached to hooks on the side of a building, then unhooked when not in use.

Use cheerful stripes, sophisticated dark tones, soothing pale shades or vibrant right-between-the-eyes colours depending on the look of your space. Small mirrors, like the ones used in Indian fabrics, sewn onto the underside of an awning would twinkle delightfully at night. Instead of choosing a tough fabric, you could try woven matting (perhaps reed or split bamboo) for an organic, natural look, or sheer voile for its airy delicacy.

beams and wires

Use simple spans of interesting materials (such as monumental iron girders, ancient reclaimed beams, slim metal struts, colourful plastic tubing or delicate metal wires) for a minimalist overhead structure, but pick a material that suits your space. Slim overheads won't cut out the light, while heavy beams could support a hammock or swing-seat.

GARDEN FURNITURE

If you can squeeze into your garden, it's big enough to contain some sort of furniture. Make yourself comfortable outside; your outdoor room should be inviting and useful, a place to laze around and enjoy life. Install a stool on a tiny balcony, sling a hammock between an old tree and a well-placed post, push an armchair out through the French windows or, for low-level lounging, carry plenty of cushions and rugs outside.

Choose furniture that fits in with the style of your outdoor space. There's a wide variety of seating and tables that would work outside, so don't buy dull wooden items just because that's what they have in your local garden centre. Unless furniture is for purely decorative purposes, it should be comfortable, particularly if you plan to use it a lot. Don't be shy: settle yourself down in chairs and loungers while they are still in the shop.

Built-in furniture is great for saving space and for impromptu sorties when the sun appears from behind the clouds: just wipe off the rain. When walls are built, think ahead. Should they be made wider/higher/lower so they can also double up as benches? (A double-thickness brick retaining wall at least 50 cm (19 in) high will do well for seating.) Custom-made fitted cushions complete the design and can easily be put in place

on built-in seating when the weather permits. If you've got limited space, folding furniture can be stashed away when not in use. Extending tables expand or contract to match the size of your party. Benches are good for enthusiastic socialites (as long as your guests don't mind squeezing up) and stools can double up as plant stands. Tables may be used to display plants, or you can use them to do the potting when you aren't eating alfresco. In a really small

space, permanent furniture might be a bad idea: just carry indoor items outside when you need them. Swinging seats lend an air of luxury to an outdoor space: add linen or cashmere cushions for total opulence. Sun loungers are the ultimate for comfort. Finally, a seat around a tree is a lovely idea and it looks charming when it is not being used.

Paint furniture to match flowers, containers or trellis (a cheap pine bench will look gorgeous painted pale mauve and surrounded by lavender).

Improvise and create furniture that isn't purpose-built: try a sturdy log, a rounded boulder or an old beer barrel with a cushion on top – a place to sit needn't cost a thing. For a final touch, get cushions, pads and mattresses. Use indoor favourites or make new ones to fit your garden furniture. Have blocks of foam cut to size and cover them in stretch towelling, ticking or robust canvas.

wooden furniture

Wooden furniture fits well in a garden. Good hardwood furniture, including teak and iroko, is expensive, but wonderfully solid and it lasts a lifetime. It can be left out and will weather to an elegant silvery grey. Make sure any hardwood comes from a renewable source. Softwood furniture needs annual painting or treatment with preservative or it should be stored inside in the winter months. Built-in wooden furniture can be made from planks of decking. So, if you're decking the floor, consider incorporating benches and tables into the design for a refined, uniform look. A smooth block of wood could make a stylish table, stool or plant stand. Furniture made in slim branches of wood, with the bark kept on, looks attractively rustic – the uneven quality of the wood adds to its appeal. Finally, cheap wooden furniture can be smartened up with a coat of varnish or paint.

wicker

Plain wicker is redolent of colonial days. Exotic, yet natural in effect, it would look great in a garden with tropical planting. Painted white or pastel, wicker is utterly romantic.

plastic, perspex and resin

Cheap plastic furniture is good for temporary use and can be painted in fun colours. It's also light (which makes it a good choice for roof gardens or balconies) and rotproof, so it can be left outside permanently. Designer plastic or Perspex (Plexiglass) furniture, complete with a huge price tag, can give a superbly glamorous feel. Virtually invisible, clear Perspex is great for a minimalist look. Resin furniture tends to be stronger and more durable than plastic. Folding chairs and tables made of resin are light and easy to move around.

metal

Modern cast-metal furniture is often hideous (and best restricted to beer gardens). Antique examples can be elegantly ornate. Watch out, though: they're often extremely uncomfortable. Wrought-iron furniture can be deeply traditional or bizarrely futuristic, and it's usually expensive. Tubular steel is light and modern, but the joints may rust, so it's not ideal for leaving outside. Wire furniture varies from old-fashioned, ornate and romantic to sparse and contemporary. It is delicate and won't appear cumbersome in a small space.

stone

Stone and reconstituted stone furniture can be impressive and weighty. Antique examples give a traditional, timeless air to a space, but they are not cheap. Smooth, modern designs in natural stone may look marvellous, but are likely to be very expensive. Off-the-shelf reconstituted stone furniture, such as curved benches, can be difficult to site where it will blend in well – unless you have opted for a country mansion look.

fabric

If you haven't got a suitable tree, buy a hammock with its own stand and relive that week in the Caribbean (or favourite movie). For a seaside feel, deck chairs are jolly and inexpensive, and director's chairs, although they can't be left outside, can easily be carried out (the cheaper ones have an unfortunate habit of collapsing, though).

LIGHTING

An astute investment in a garden, lighting can transform an outdoor space into a magical Arcadia or a mysterious under-world. And, of course, it extends the time you can enjoy and use your garden: when you're forced to stay inside on winter evenings, a beautifully lit outside space provides a great backdrop. When the weather is warm, you can linger outside long into the night.

There's a variety of lights for different effects: check out spotlights, recessed wall and floor lights, floodlights, uplighters, downlighters, fibre-optic lights, bollard lights, underwater lights, coloured lights, pendants, candles (garden candles often contain citronella to deter insects), flares and lanterns.

If the light fixtures will be visible during the day, look for attractive examples that will blend in with the style of your garden. A gothic cast-iron lantern won't look good in a modern minimalist space, but recessed aluminium floor lights might be perfect.

Don't stop at the mundane: chandeliers, fairy lights, lasers, paper lanterns and gaudy plastic lights are fun and bring sparkle. At night, theatrical effects, which would look tawdry by day, can be employed. You could even use a projector to throw pictures or colourful patterns onto walls or screens.

A purely functional bright light from a single source flattens and deadens the garden at night. To create mystery and interest, use various different lighting techniques to illuminate certain features while leaving other areas of the garden dark. Move lights around to find the best place for them and so unattractive functional lights are hidden. Experiment with changes in mood and atmosphere and alter the lighting to emphasize the changing garden scene.

spotlights and backlight

Use spotlights to highlight interesting objects or focal points: simply shine a fairly concentrated beam away from the viewpoint onto the object.

Don't use too many spotlights or the drama will be lost (one or two will do). Use backlighting for fascinating silhouettes. You should direct a light from close behind an object, but make sure the light itself isn't visible. This effect looks great in winter with bare trees and shrubs, particularly those with interesting, twisted shapes.

uplighters or downlighters?

Use uplighters or downlighters to illuminate a single feature. You can shine a fairly narrow beam up or down it; this technique works especially well for tall structures like trees or columns. Uplighters with a wider beam cast a surreal glow up from the earth. Diffuse, pure white downlighters can be used to simulate moonlight, but use a fairly weak light source to avoid a harsh, unnatural effect. Site them high in a tree or above an overhead structure for 'moon' shadows on the ground. Use grazing light to emphasize the texture of a wall, fence or tree. To do this, position a light at the base so that its beam just brushes over the surface, picking up the pattern.

illuminating water

Spectacular effects can be produced by illuminating water. Fountains look truly wonderful glittering in the dark, so try placing a spotlight beneath or behind the water spray. Floating lights will twinkle prettily on the water's surface. On a still night, you could use candles for this effect. Underwater lights give an unearthly air: experiment with an array of different colours to achieve different atmospheres. Site a light behind a plant near a still pool to create mysterious shadows on the water's surface.

candles and flares

For special occasions, flares lining a path or surrounding a table have a medieval feel. Small candles dotted around the garden will create the effect of a starry night. You can use storm lanterns or empty jars to protect candles from breezes.

lanterns

Lanterns needn't hang above a door: suspend them from sturdy branches or arching bamboo sticks, or try a row of Chinese paper lanterns hanging along a string. Oil lamps can be picked up in antique and secondhand

shops – their flickering light is very atmospheric – or you could push Thai bamboo garden lamps into a clump of architectural foliage to look like exotic, luminous flowers.

functional lights

Floodlights make good utility lights and can be used to illuminate large areas. Lighting that comes on as you approach the front door is useful as it may deter burglars and means you can quickly get your key in the lock late at night. For paths and steps, use low-level

lighting. (This will help make sure no one trips up, but it won't highlight them.) These lights can be built into the side walls of steps or simply be positioned alongside them.

practicalities

Always employ a professional electrician to install garden lighting. When there's water around and the possibility of hitting a cable with your trowel, it is dangerous to play with electricity yourself. It's safest to use a low-voltage system that is connected to a transformer and a circuit breaker indoors.

WATER

Water adds another dimension to a garden. Particularly valuable in a small garden, it's a great way to enliven a restricted area and make it more interesting. Reflections in still pools bring the sky down, increasing the light and feeling of space. Moving water gurgles and rushes, drowning out the sound of traffic and heightening the sense of a lush paradise. Informal ponds encourage wildlife – you'll be amazed how quickly the frogs find your watery delight.

For glints of burnished gold, introduce fish (in an urban garden they are less likely to be eaten by herons than their rural counterparts). Water is the ultimate element to help you relax and unwind: its soothing noise and the play of light on its surface give a great feeling of peace.

One word of warning: even very shallow water can be hazardous with small children around. Make sure they are never left unattended near an open water feature. If you've got children (or have visitors with children),

make your garden completely child-friendly by erecting a fence around the water feature or have a sturdy metal grille made to fit over the surface until they grow up and are no longer in danger of falling into the water.

And finally, don't forget to illuminate your water feature. Fantastic, spectacular or just plain pretty effects can all be easily achieved (see lighting, pages 124–5).

still pools and ponds

Wonderfully tranquil in effect, even the most simple still pool brings life and variety to a garden. A beautiful basin filled with water is an easy option.

Leave it unplanted to provide a point of calm. Grow a miniature water lily in an ordinary pot (seal any drainage holes with silicone aquarium sealant) and it becomes quite magical. Or, for a tiny nature reserve, a half-barrel or an old ceramic or stone sink can be filled with a mix of aquatic plants.

Pools and ponds can have very different characters. A geometric pool surrounded by smooth paving is formal and controlled, whereas a curvy, asymmetrical pond with lush, marginal planting is more wild. For a seamless, uncluttered look, create a pool that has its water level flush with the surrounding paving. Planting overhanging pool

PLANTING

Grow submerged and marginal pond plants in planting baskets that contain special aquatic compost (soil) topped with a layer of gravel. Floating plants simply float on the water's surface: try water hyacinth (*Eichhornia crassipes*), water lettuce (*Pistia stratiotes*) (these are both not hardy and should be overwintered indoors) or the slightly tender fairy moss (*Azolla filiculoides*).

CREATING A POND

To make your own pond, dig a hole to the depth you require, then remove any sharp stones. Line the base with pond underlay and then spread a flexible butyl pond liner over the underlay. Allow at least 15 cm (6 in) extra of liner and underlay to overlap the edge of the hole. Use tent stakes to hold down the overlap and lay decking or stone slabs around the edge of the pond to hide the stakes and excess liner. Allow the deck or stone to overhang the water slightly to conceal the lined sides of the pond. Add a selection of aquatic plants (see stylish water plants, page 130, and check correct planting depths at your garden centre). You could also install a fountain, then fill your pond with water and enjoy.

margins imparts a mysterious air and makes shadow patterns on the water's surface. The bottom of a shallow pool could be decorated for a novel effect: try arranging a spiral of contrasting pebbles or crushed glass on it.

Dye the water in a still pool black or use a black pool liner to create fantastic reflections of clouds and overhanging plants. If you plan to hold lots of parties, install a raised pool. These have walls around their edges that can double up as extra seating, saving precious space. (Make sure the edges are high and wide enough to be comfortable.) Place cushions on the walls for comfort and watch your friends unwind as they trail their hands through the cool water.

A shallow pebble pond lined with pebbles and cobblestones is easy to make and would fit in well if you've used cobble-stones or pebbles elsewhere in the garden. Site it in shade so the water doesn't become horribly green. Or look for instant pond kits that can be assembled quickly and placed directly on the terrace (no digging required). They can be improved by painting or staining the

wooden side panels or by attaching sheets of shiny metal. With any pool, make sure the waterproof liner is not visible around the edges or the magic will be lost.

hot tubs

If you want to lounge about in water, go for a hot tub. They are far cheaper than a swimming pool and will not take up too much space (you could even install one on the roof for Hollywood-style glamour). Perfect for romantic evenings, they are also a fun alternative to a child's blow-up paddling pool.

moving water

Choose from an array of delightful moving-water effects, from foaming jets, bubbling springs and gushing spouts to sparkling fountains. Simply use a submersible electric pump to get your water on the move.

FOUNTAINS

Check out the huge range of fountain heads and nozzles now available. Visit an aquatic centre to see the best selection and ask them to demonstrate what your fountain (and pump) will look like when working. Lots of small holes produce a fine

FISH

Fish will certainly add zest to a water feature and, as pets go, they are pretty easy to look after (goldfish are probably the easiest). To keep fish happy and healthy, grow submerged (oxygenating) plants, feed them the right amount and make sure they are sheltered from the sun (fish can actually get sunburnt). A couple of small fish could even be housed in a large urn (choose one with a wide opening to give the fish more oxygen) and make sure the water doesn't freeze over. To prevent freezing, use a floating pond heater. If the water does freeze over, rest a hot cup on the surface of the ice to make a hole in it (fish may be traumatized if you smash the ice with a hammer).

Fish will benefit from a fountain (particularly one with a fine spray), which helps to oxygenate the water. Fish food and fish droppings introduce nutrients into the water which allow algae to thrive, so turning the water green. Combat this with a selection of water plants that will compete with the algae for nutrients (and provide shade for the fish, too).

MURKY WATER: ALL YOU NEED TO KNOW

If you wanted a limpid, crystalline pool and you've ended up with green soup, here's what to do. Green water is caused by millions of green algae floating in the water. Algae won't flourish in the shade, so one solution is to site your water feature in a shady place. Alternatively, grow plants with large leaves, such as water lilies, which shade the surface of the water.

Introduce a few oxygenating (submerged) and floating plants into the water. These will compete with the algae for nutrients and help keep the water clear. However, some pools look best without any plants. For these you will need an ultra-violet filter, which reduces algae, or you can buy chemical solutions to add to small water features.

Green water is not a problem in features that have a dark (concealed or underground) water reservoir, where the algae cannot thrive. So, if you want clear water, you could opt for a bubble fountain or a wall-mounted fountain with its reservoir hidden under stones.

spray, whereas larger ones make more obvious water jets. Different fixtures can be used to create a single, narrow plume of water, a rosette of jets spreading outwards in a circle or tiers of cascading water of different heights.

A bell or dome fountain makes a miraculous film of water that sweeps down from the nozzle (install it in a sheltered spot so the film remains intact). Geyser nozzles mix water and air to produce an exuberant foaming jet. They are especially good for small water features – the water tends to remain in them because it isn't propelled as far – and they also work well in a pond with fish because they aerate the water.

For a spectacular effect, try a rotating fountain, which revolves to create sinuous arcs of water in the air. Rather more low-key, a jet placed underwater makes a subtle ripple or bubble on the water's surface. Don't forget: fountains needn't be huge – a small one could fit comfortably into a large dish.

A fountain head can also be a feature in its own right, rather than just a functional nozzle.

For modern gardens, avoid the ubiquitous cherub. Look for a cutting-edge design or make your own from contemporary materials such as plastic, metal sheeting, piping or anything else that appeals to you.

ON THE WALL

A wall fountain is another option for moving water. These have a wall-mounted spout or mask from which water tumbles into a vessel below, to then be pumped back up. They can be squeezed into the tiniest space (even a balcony) and will spice up the garden. You can buy all-in-one versions that simply

attach to the wall or you could assemble your own using anything that allows a stream of water to flow through or along it, such as an old piece of pipe, a salvaged stone gargoyle, a section of an iron girder or a beautiful pre-drilled shell, secured on the wall above a reservoir to catch the water below. You can make the reservoir into a feature in its own right or hide it underneath stones through which the water trickles (the latter would be child-safe). Wall fountains look great encircled by climbers; this can integrate them into the rest of the garden.

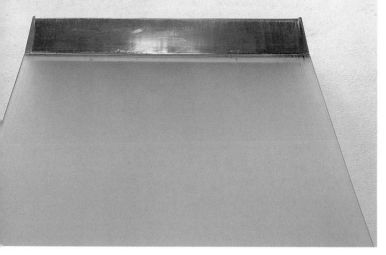

different spouts and containers: the possibilities are limitless. But do make sure the noise created by your water feature is pleasant and soothing, and not like the irritating sound of a tap (faucet) left running. If necessary, place stones under the stream to improve the sound.

In a modern garden, you could construct a 'wall' of water running down a panel of stainless steel or glass for a dynamic effect. This could be freestanding or wall-mounted. For a hefty price, you can get glass spheres (aquaspheres), which shimmer miraculously as water flows endlessly over the surface. Alternatively, water flowing over a slab of stone or a chiselled monolith would beautifully enhance it.

RILLS

A rill is a channel of water resembling a tiny canal. It can be used to delineate an area of the garden or simply to create patterns on the ground. Rills look excellent in formal gardens; flowing water enlivens the static design. The water can be left open, or overhung so it is only partially visible (and child-safe). Rills can be constructed with level changes for mini-waterfalls.

OFF THE WALL

A bubble fountain is a good option if you want something subtle and child-safe. Site the fountain head in a collection of stones and pebbles (and any other materials you like) so that the water bubbles up over them, giving them an attractive sheen, cooling the air and making a pleasant gurgle. A hidden reservoir under the stones collects the water and contains a pump that recycles the water back up to the fountain head.

For a variation on a bubble fountain, circulate water through a brimming pot or urn so that it constantly overflows onto stones below. Place the pot upright so the water trickles down its sides, making them gleam. Water returns to the pot via a flexible tube threaded through a hole in the base.

In a Japanese-style garden, water could be circulated through a bamboo spout teamed with a granite bowl. For a different look, you could run water along a row of the same containers (each one placed slightly lower than the one before to catch the water from it). Get creative with

PUMPS

For most small fountains, a pump rated at 1,000 litres (300 gallons) per hour is suitable. If you want something more eye-catching, get a more powerful pump, but don't go overboard with a small water feature or the pump will squirt all the water out of it. (The water should fall back into the pool or reservoir to be recycled.) Rotating fountains require a pump of at least 3,000 or 4,000 litres (800 or 1,000 gallons) per hour.

INSTALLING AND MAINTAINING A FOUNTAIN AND PUMP

Position your pump on a slab clear of the pond silt with the top of the fountain head just above the water. Use a water-proof plug to plug the pump's electric cable into a proper outdoor power socket installed by a professional electrician. Alternatively, get an electrician to install a transformer to reduce the electricity supply to a low-voltage supply that can be safely used outdoors. Check and clean the filter regularly; you'll soon get to know how often it silts up. If the fountain nozzle becomes blocked, clean it with a solution of vinegar.

STYLISH WATER PLANTS

- Water lilies (*Nymphaea*): Exquisite flowers are framed by round pads on the water's surface. Choose a variety that remains open when you want to see them. Using a single colour works best: white is elegant; red, yellow and pink are also available. Don't place a fountain nearby, as they don't like turbulence or having their leaves sprayed.

- Horsetail rush (*Equisetum*) (above left): Outlandish, pre-historic plant with slim, leafless stems notched by brown bands.

- Arum lily (*Zantedeschia aethiopica* 'Crowborough'): Sculpted white flowers with a yellow spike. Grow these style icons in boggy soil or in water.

- Water irises: These, and yellow and blue flag irises, all thrive in shallow water.

- Umbrella grass (*Cyperus involucratus*) (above right): An architectural plant with leaves like umbrella spokes at the end of long, slim stems. Not hardy, overwinter indoors.

- Club rush/Zebra rush (*Schoenoplectus lacustris* subsp. *tabernaemontani* 'Zebrinus'): Funky stripes cross its leaves. It spreads easily and needs to be cut back annually.

- Skunk cabbage (*Lysichiton americanus*): Spectacular yellow flowers have an unpleasant smell.

- Variegated water grass (*Glyceria maxima* var. *variegata*): Chic, with cream- and white-striped green leaves. Spreads quickly.

MOISTURE-LOVING PLANTS

These go perfectly beside water in damp soil; they will relish the cool atmosphere.

- Day lilies (*Hemerocallis*): Beautiful, trumpet-shaped flowers in a range of colours.

- Iris: Their elegant leaves and flowers look fabulous reflected in water. Good types to grow in moist soil include *Iris sibirica* and *Iris ensata*.

- Hostas: These have broad, handsome leaves. Some have sculptural ridges, while others have white or yellow patterns.

- Umbrella plant (*Darmera peltata*): As the name suggests, this plant has large, umbrella-like leaves.

- Grasses: Use these to contrast with wide-leaved plants. Grow Bowles' golden sedge (*Carex elata* 'Aurea') and pendulous sedge (*Carex pendula*).

- Ferns: Try the splendid regal fern (*Osmunda regalis*) if you've got plenty of space.

OUTDOOR ART & SCULPTURE

Sculpture and other artworks look superb in a garden and give the space an edge. You could choose a piece that links with your indoor style. A sculpture can throw the planting into dramatic relief or, for a more subtle look, echo surrounding leaf or plant shapes. A mobile of clear plastic discs would imitate the flat, round seedpods of honesty (*Lunaria*). Forget run-of-the-mill sculpture and go for something abstract, kitsch or monumental.

A sculpture can provide a focal point at the end of a vista or one could be used as a surprise element around a corner. Add a touch of humour by placing sculptures where they tie in – an old wooden decoy duck in the rushes by a pond, a sphinx guarding a gateway or a file of gnomes marching off around a corner might be just what's needed.

figures

The human form can be the most effective sculpture in a garden. Figures can 'people' the space, create mystery or surprise and be marvellously gruesome and eerie. Try a bust peering out from foliage, a pair of feet sticking out of the earth or an arm hanging from a tree.

animals

Some animal sculptures are horribly tasteless, but some will look perfect (or humorous). Don't overdo it or your meditative oasis will turn into a zoo. Look for animals and figures shaped from stone, wire, metal, willow twigs, rushes, clay or reclaimed wood.

abstract

Even in a small space, huge artworks, which you'd never find space for indoors, can be indulged in. Organic shapes can mimic nature, while crisp geometry can provide a foil. These artworks do not have to be expensive: a smooth boulder, a cragged rock, a contorted branch, a stretch of chicken wire, a piece of twisted iron, glass bricks or a sheet of corrugated plastic can all make something interesting.

found objects

An old engine, a reclaimed angel or a gargoyle could introduce a touch of irony. Try architectural salvage yards or scrap merchants for interesting pieces.

birdbaths and sundials

If they fit the setting, these can look good. Most are in very traditional designs, though.

living sculptures

Clip plants such as box into a whole range of topiary shapes (see page 98), or mould chicken wire to create a shape, then push it in a pot of soil and train a small-leaved ivy over it to form a close green covering over the wire.

obelisks and urns

Use these as focal points or to flank a door or path. Antique versions can be very costly.

wall art

Consider murals, mosaics, wall sculptures and wall plaques (which take up little space and can be framed with climbers).

ACCESSORIES & TOOLS

Give your garden its own individual style with a few well-chosen accessories. Finding useful and decorative items for your outside space is lots of fun. Choose objects that tie in with what's already outside and that will reinforce the theme or style of your garden.

Try to find functional objects that are aesthetic, too. Hunt for stylish watering cans, textiles, pots, lanterns, plant supports and labels; you'll be surprised what a variety is on offer. Don't overlook recycled and reclaimed objects: their non-pristine looks fit well outdoors. These final touches bring a space to life, giving it an appealing lived-in feel. Experiment and enjoy yourself. Here are some ideas you could consider:

barbecues and outdoor ovens

Being outside makes cooking and eating fun. For easy living, get a barbecue or an outdoor oven. All you need to do is place the food on it (well, almost). So decamp to the garden and hold those supper parties outside.

Don't bother with a built-in barbecue in a small garden: a portable one can be wheeled out of sight when the sleet sets in. For an instant barbie, pile up a few bricks on a spare paving slab and place an oven shelf across the top. Terracotta ovens provide different cooking opportunities and can also look decorative.

plant stands

Prevent your space from looking flat and monotonous by using plant stands to get plants off the ground. Try some of the following options:

* Delicate Victorian wirework jardinières – these look pretty and are perfect for displaying a romantic jumble of herbs (see below), trailing

geraniums, helichrysum, verbena and petunias. They can be expensive, so shop around at auctions of garden furniture and raid junk stores for bargains.

- Kits of tiered metal shelves are available from many garden centres and mail-order catalogues. Use rectangular versions along a wall or quarter circles in corners. Paint them to match other garden accessories or to complement the flowers.
- Use a wooden or metal stepladder as an instant plant stand. You could display the same type of plant all the way up, or use it for pots of herbs and stand it near the kitchen door for easy access.
- Raise pots above ground level by standing them on planks supported by bricks, flowerpots or logs. Paint or stain the planks in a colour that looks good with the planting and the pots.
- Go grand – cheap modern clay pipes (or chimney pots) can be set upright to form superb columns to place plants on top. The terracotta versions will soon weather and look better with age (see rapid ageing, page 138). In the meantime, grow trailing plants to veil them.
- Look for plant holders that are specially designed to attach small single pots to posts or walls.

heaters and outdoor fireplaces

A freestanding patio heater is a sound investment in colder climates and, if you're planning to have a meal outside, you can guarantee that your guests will be comfortable, too. Heaters can look good, create a cosy circle of warmth and are easy to use as they run off gas canisters. Alternatively, get an outdoor 'fireplace'. These range from a metal basket for laying a fire inside (a cheaper but less effective and more time-consuming option) to a charming, dumpy terracotta 'chiminea' for a rustic effect.

finishing touches

Complete your garden room with some (or all) of the following:

- **Parasols**: These provide welcome cool shade in hot weather and look appealing over a dining table.

(see rapid ageing, page 138)

Before you start work, get properly equipped to make life easier. You will need:

- For digging and weeding: A spade, fork, trowel and other tools specially designed to take the strain out of weeding (check out your garden centre).
- Watering cans: Buy one with a fine rose sprinkler head for delicate plants (look for chic, modern versions that are good enough to tempt even non-plant owners). A hose may make watering easier.
- Plant labels: Don't leave ugly plastic labels on your plants (you wouldn't want the price tag dangling off your new shirt, would you?) Either write down what you've bought in a book reserved for your gardening notes or invest in some attractive labels in copper, terracotta, slate or steel.
- Shears for trimming hedges and secateurs (clippers) for pruning.
- Twine for training climbing plants. Plastic-coated wire is more convenient, but it may cut stems.
- Buckets, gloves, a broom or brush, plant food and spray, and bird-friendly slug pellets.
- Protect tender plants with horticultural fleece or cloches, from smooth glass or plastic bells to Victorian lead-framed mini-greenhouse lookalikes.

- **Textiles**: Buy floral fabrics so you can still have flowers in the garden when yours aren't blooming. Linen and cotton fabrics are suitably hard-wearing and natural. When you're eating outside, do it in style. Don't just rush out with a handful of knives and forks; make it a sumptuous experience with crisp tablecloths and napkins.

- **Plant supports**: Use elegant silver spirals, twiggy branches or functional wire shapes.

- **Wind chimes**: Beware – their noise can be totally infuriating. Look for bamboo or terracotta types for a muted mellow sound, rather than tinkly metal.

- Take photographs of your favourite flowers and have them printed on mugs so you can enjoy your garden in the middle of winter.

- Topiary frames are decorative even if you can't be bothered to neatly snip plants to fit them; try growing small climbers over them instead.

- Stone balls, glass beads, blankets, salvaged millstones, plant trolleys, bird tables and feeders: all of these can decorate your space.

BUILDINGS

In many gardens, there isn't much room for big structures, but a small building might provide a brilliant extra living space, a rain retreat, a storage room or even just a decorative feature. The options include:

garden sheds

These are generally cheap, utilitarian and extremely useful. They can be transformed with imaginative painting or almost hidden by vigorous climbers.

gazebos

Gazebos are open-sided buildings designed for gazing out from. They can make an attractive focal point, but provide little shelter from the elements. A gazebo might be fun on a roof where spectacular views could be enjoyed, but you may need to contact the relevant planning authorities in your area.

summerhouses

These are mini-houses that can be used for eating, reading and any other activities you do in your home. As they are often a major investment, don't bother to buy one if you won't make the most of it and all you really want is somewhere for storage. Most ready-made designs are very traditional in style and wouldn't work in a modern garden.

treehouses

Treehouses provide lots of fun for children. A suitable tree can be helped with freestanding posts. Into the bargain, they don't take up precious floor space. You could build a top-of-the-range model and use it as an outdoor office.

mini-marquees

If you plan to entertain outside regularly and the weather is unpredictable, it may be worth investing in a custom-made marquee (tent) that perfectly fits your roof, balcony or terrace. Have it made so the sides can be rolled up when it is warm.

greenhouses

Greenhouses are worthwhile if you are a plant addict and want to be out there, no matter what the weather. Make yours an even more pleasant place to be with a comfortable chair and pretty cushions.

IRRIGATION

for containers

Without an irrigation system, on sunny days you may be labouring with a watering can, when you would prefer to be relaxing with a drink. (It can take over an hour a day to water a collection of pots.) Invest in a dripper system – most of these are fairly easy to install – to help you avoid this daily hot-weather chore.

Attach a timer to an outdoor tap (faucet) and connect it to a piece of hose running close to all your plant containers. For each container, puncture the hose with a dripper and run a piece of spaghetti pipe from the dripper to the container (use several drippers for large containers). Stake the end of the spaghetti pipe in place with a plastic spike, then preset the timer to water the plants first thing in the morning and/or at night. Monitor the results and adjust the flow or the length of watering time to get damp (but not sodden) soil. If you really are organized (and enjoy slavish routine), you could just attach a hose to the kitchen tap. When you've got more than a few pots to water, this will make the job much easier than using a watering can.

for the main garden

Even if your plants will survive without irrigation, they will be happier if they are watered. In urban gardens particularly, the soil can be extremely dry because buildings create shelter from the rain and masonry absorbs water from the soil. In all but the most damp and shady spots, irrigation is a worthwhile investment. A porous pipe system is fine for most gardens, and isn't too expensive. High-tech sprinklers are not necessary unless you like gadgets or are obsessed with your lawn. To install the system, lay porous pipe on the surface of the soil near your plants, spacing the lengths about 50–60 cm (20–40 in) apart. Bury them with a layer of bark, compost or soil. Run a normal (non-porous) hose from the garden tap to the area you want to water and connect it to the porous pipe. This system can be turned on and off manually, or by using a timer on the tap.

PLANT CONTAINERS

Containers allow you to exploit every inch of outdoor space. Perch them on a window ledge, install them by the front door, hang them on a wall, or line them up along a passageway. Smaller containers can be easily moved about: put them centre stage when they're full of flowers, then whisk them away when they've faded, or switch them around occasionally for new colour combinations. Large containers provide greater planting possibilities (including trees) and don't dry out so fast in hot weather. If you live in an area where there is a possibility that your containers might be stolen, choose large, heavy ones (that will be even heavier when filled with soil) to deter burglars.

Use the same planters indoors and out (perhaps placed in a continuous line) to blur the boundaries between the two spaces, turning them into a single coherent living space. A row of matching containers up a flight of steps looks fun and creates a feeling of rhythm, while a pair of elegant containers flanking a door lends an impressive air. Avoid grouping masses of small pots on the ground: they will only look cluttered and take up valuable floor space. Move small potted plants off the floor to where they can be admired; use plant stands or place them on tables or shelves (plants at different heights make the space more interesting, too). For a stylish and inexpensive display, grow a packet of easy annuals and pot them in a row of identical containers along a window ledge or shelf: try pot marigolds, nasturtiums or violas.

Hang wall containers on trellises using butcher's 'S' hooks (no drilling is required) or place a large, attractive container (planted or empty) in a flower bed as a focal point. Hanging baskets are a matter of taste (a big ball of colourful flowers can look rather unnatural) and the soil dries out quickly. For a novel effect, look for high-tech floating containers.

Select containers to fit in with the setting. Smooth, pale concrete works well in contemporary spaces; hewn granite would look good if you opt for a Japanese-style garden. Weathered stone works in traditional settings and transparent plastic in futuristic ones. You could use materials that are already present elsewhere in your home, indoors or out. Terracotta pots would look good with terracotta tiles, and galvanized pots would blend in with grey-leaved plants (see below).

When it comes to sourcing containers for plants, the choice is endless. Standard options include terracotta pots, stone troughs, lead tanks, wooden half-barrels, plastic pots and boxes, galvanized metal buckets, glazed pots, wooden boxes and fibre pots. But don't feel you need to buy your planters from a garden centre. More interesting containers can often be found elsewhere (and

may be far cheaper, too). Trawl through junk shops, flea markets, family attics and kitchen cupboards. Unless you are going for a deliberately cluttered look, avoid using too many different types of container. Go for one or two styles in different sizes. Stone and terracotta look good together but galvanized steel and rubber might look right in a contemporary setting.

planting

Some pots are best unplanted. Leave olive jars and other pots with narrow necks empty: they look far better without plants crammed into the small planting space. Neat stacks of empty terracotta pots can also look decorative, so don't feel you have to store them away.

When planting annuals (which only last for a season) in a container, really cram them in for a luxuriant display. Nothing looks more pathetic than a few tiny plants in a big box of soil. When a potted plant is past its best, throw it out and buy something new. After all, expensive bunches of flowers have a shelf-life, so don't get sentimental about last year's Christmas poinsettia. You needn't grow a mixture of plants in a large pot: a number of identical plants might look more stylish.

terracotta

These are unglazed (usually orange-red in colour) earthy pots, boxes and urns. They can be expensive (antique and elaborately decorated ones are frighteningly so), but they improve with age. Machine-made flower pots have a stylish, no-nonsense look. Left plain, they look good arranged in a row, or you could paint them in a solid colour or stripes or spots. Long Toms are straight-sided and more elegant. Terracotta is not just available in orange-red: faience is a cream-coloured form and you can also find a warm, yellowish Cretan terracotta (Ali Baba jars and flat pans) and dark brown pots. Before you leave them outside over winter, check that they are frostproof, or they may crack. Line their sides with plastic sheeting to reduce water loss in hot weather as they are porous.

stone

Natural stone is a quality material which gives a great

DRAINAGE

You can use just about anything to grow plants in. All a container needs is a few holes to drain the water away so the roots of the plants don't sit in it. (Most plants, apart from bog and aquatic types, hate having their roots in standing water.) If your container hasn't any drainage holes, get your drill out and make some.

To improve drainage, a container should also have a layer of drainage material in the bottom. If there's room, use about a 3-cm (1-in) layer (or more in large containers). Buy leica or leitag (being light, this is good for use in pots on balconies or roof terraces) or use bits of broken terracotta, gravel, stones or even chunks of polystyrene (styrofoam). If your container is on a flat surface, it may be worth raising it off the ground for better drainage. You can buy specially designed pot 'feet', but chunks of brick or tile work just as well.

RAPID AGEING

Terracotta pots generally look better when they're old. Paint new ones with live (bio) yoghurt to speed up the ageing process (they will whiten in direct sunlight and become greener if they are left in the shade). Repeat the process for stubbornly fresh pots.

wood

There are various options for wooden containers:

- Wooden half-barrels are useful for growing larger plants and even small trees.
- Natural-wood boxes can have marvellous graining. They combine well with plants and look good outdoors. You could visit a quality wine shop and ask if they have any spare wooden wine or port cases (they make great containers).
- Versailles tubs are based on a historic French design (used in Louis XIV's palace, the Château de Versailles) and have a traditional feel. They are often used for citrus trees or topiary such as clipped box or bay plants. Well-made hardwood versions are expensive.
- Marine plywood boxes are fairly resilient and cheap. They should last at least five years outside and look best painted or stained.
- Look for window boxes made from wood with the bark left on for a rustically kitsch effect, or create your own natural container from a hollowed-out log.

feeling of permanence, but antique stone troughs and even modern versions can be very expensive. Look for good reproduction stone containers instead, or lava pots, which are attractively modern and more affordable.

concrete

Concrete can be very beautiful and may fit perfectly in a modern setting. Some concrete reproduction stone is very convincing and ages beautifully, but avoid poor quality reproduction stone which is unattractive and will still look brand new 20 years later. You can find bizarre Edwardian concrete rusticana (the Edwardians were great enthusiasts of concrete) in the shape of log pots and troughs that are quirky and kitsch.

glazed

Generally imported from the Far East, glazed pots often look good with Eastern plants such as bamboo and Japanese maples. Dark blue and green finishes are subtle, while bright cobalt blue can look good in a sunny Mediterranean or California-style space.

fibre

Fibre pots are used for growing seeds and are simply buried in the ground with the plant. They are attractively natural and functional, but don't last long.

metal

Contemporary, bright and durable, galvanized steel is very shiny when new; the finish eventually dulls to look less obvious. Window boxes and florist's buckets are most commonly available. For custom-made troughs, visit an air-conditioning ducting supplier – often they'll make some for you. This is a cheap way of getting large containers that perfectly fit your space. They may also have circular ducting that can be cut to make sections to cover cheap pots. Galvanized steel containers work well in modern gardens and they could be painted for more subtle (or glaringly colourful) effects. They may rust along the joints or edges, but are reasonably weatherproof. You could use a paint kit to give cheap galvanized steel buckets a verdigris effect.

Zinc has a less shiny surface than galvanized steel. With its lovely muted look, it's good outdoors and it doesn't rust. Lead containers are a beautiful matt dark grey colour. Antique lead tanks and cisterns can cost a small fortune. New containers fashioned from lead tend to be made in traditional designs that don't work well in contemporary gardens. Lead is generally expensive and extremely heavy.

Copper looks great outdoors and weathers to a verdigris patina. Look for antique copper pans that were originally used for doing the laundry.

wire

Commonly used to make plain hanging baskets, more ornate wire containers can also be sourced. They may need to be lined (use moss, plastic, sackcloth or even old clothes) to stop the soil falling out. Or you could use a wire trough to hold other small containers. Their delicate filigree is perfect for pretty, floral gardens.

plastic

These containers come in a huge range of shapes and colours, and are usually really cheap. Paint them gorgeous colours or use black plastic for an industrial look. You could customize them by gluing items such as shells, leaves or mosaic tiles on the surface. They look great in modern gardens and, being light, they are useful for balconies and roof terraces. But mock-terracotta pots often look terrible: opt for plastic when you really want plastic.

fibreglass

You can now buy some fantastic fibreglass reproductions of terracotta, copper, stone and lead. Some versions are better than the real thing, but others still look like plastic. Fibreglass is very light and a good option on a balcony. It's also durable and low maintenance.

reclaimed and recycled containers

These can look great filled with plants: experiment with tin cans (with labels left on or removed, depending on the design), paint cans, old enamel sinks, colanders (excellent for drainage), cups, wicker baskets, wooden fruit and vegetable crates, and packing cases. Roll up strips of newspaper to make biodegradable pots (grow seeds in them and then plant them out – pot and all – after loosening the base) or coil up a chain and plant inside it.

PLANTS

Well thought-out planting gives real style to a space, whereas bad planting can look utterly hilarious. Different plants create very different atmospheres, so choose the ones that have the right feel for your garden. Would huge, jungle-like exotics or dainty pastel pretties fit in? Use plants that harmonize with one another. Plants that grow together naturally in the wild generally associate well and relish the same conditions.

Resist the impulse to buy one of every plant you like or you will end up with something resembling an upturned can of fruit salad. Plant in bold drifts for a naturalistic effect or rigid rows for geometric modernism. In general, plants look more natural in clumps of three, five or seven. Avoid pairs, unless you want to use them deliberately for symmetry (perhaps flanking a door, path or view).

Grow plants that aren't one-week wonders and include different plants for different seasons. Don't buy plants just because they look good when you visit the garden centre. The chances are that they'll shed their flowers within a week, leaving your garden deeply dull until the same time next year. In a small space, you need plants that are great performers – either long-flowering or with different seasons of interest (summer flowers and interesting bark in winter) or with lovely long-lasting foliage (leaves last longer than flowers, so make sure you have plenty of plants with attractive leaves). And don't forget evergreens for year-round appeal.

Even if you've chosen a selection of fabulous plants, the end result will be awful if they are unhappy with their growing conditions. Unless you want to mollycoddle temperamental prima donnas, opt for reliable, easy varieties that will delight in the conditions you can offer. Don't be surprised when your jungle-floor giant curls up in horror at the sun and wind on your roof, or when your Mediterranean sun-lover peters out in your gloomy basement. Get it right and your plants will flourish and look magnificent. Take note of the eventual size of a plant and how fast-growing it is. The downside of a rampant climber that quickly covers an enormous blank wall is that it may romp on to engulf the whole house, and every year you'll have to hack back sackfuls of growth to keep it under control. If you aren't prepared to carry out the maintenance, go for a slower-growing plant. Voracious house-swampers include mile-a-minute vine (this is aptly named, so proceed with caution before using this monster), Virginia creeper, Boston ivy, potato vine and *Clematis montana*.

COLOUR AND MOOD

Consider the colour of your planting, since it will affect the overall ambience. Silvery-leaved plants soothe and calm. Blues and blue-greens evoke water, creating a mood of reflection and contemplation. Yellows and oranges bring the sun into the garden, while a garden of green foliage remedies overexposure to the built environment. White lifts shady gardens out of the gloom and imparts a feeling of serenity. For visual unity, select colours that are already in the garden or inside your home.

PLANT CATEGORIES

Here is a quick guide to help you choose the right plants for your garden:

easy climbers

Some climbers need to be tied to their support but self-clinging types do the work for you (after a little initial help). Self-clingers include most ivies, Virginia creeper, Boston ivy and climbing hydrangea (see climbers for shady gardens, page 86).

- *Clematis macropetala* and *Clematis alpina*: Both are lovely clematis with dainty, bell-shaped flowers in early spring. Best of all, unlike most clematis, they don't need pruning. Look for girlie 'Markham's Pink' and starry 'White Moth'.
- *Clematis montana*: This is really easy to grow and produces an exuberant mass of blossom, but it's very vigorous, so don't grow it unless you have plenty of room (or you'll be constantly cutting it back). It suits informal gardens and will grow almost anywhere.
- Jasmine (*Jasminum officinale*): This has an exquisite fragrance, pretty flowers and dainty foliage. It is easy to grow and

doesn't need much pruning (just cut out dead stems). It makes an exuberant tangle which should be loosely tied.

- The Chilean bellflower (*Lapageria rosea*): This is easy if grown somewhere sunny and sheltered (it's quite tender). It is evergreen with exotic-looking flowers, slow-growing and doesn't need pruning but does need tying up.
- Blue passion flower (*Passiflora caerulea*) (near right): This isn't very hardy but should be happy in a warm city garden. Its bizarre flowers look like a cross between an exotic insect and a satellite dish. It doesn't need pruning (just cut out dead stems) but needs tying up.
- Star jasmine (*Trachelospermum jasminoides*): This has glossy evergreen leaves and pure white summer flowers. This is a great plant for warmer gardens as it's fairly tender.
- Potato vines: *Solanum crispum* and *Solanum jasminoides* 'Album') bear a mass of attractive flowers in white or purple. They're easy to grow but vigorous.

jungle plants

- Japanese hardy banana (*Musa basjoo*): This is pretty tough as bananas go and should be

fine in a reasonably sheltered garden. It has huge leaves, which sway in the breeze like splendid banners. Give it plenty of water and fertilizer. If you wrap the trunk in sacking in winter, it will carry on growing from the top the following spring (if you don't, it may die back to ground-level in cold conditions).

- Palms: The Chusan palm (*Trachycarpus fortunei*) (above far right) and the Mediterranean fan palm (*Chamaerops humilis*) are widely available. Look for the Mexican blue palm (*Brahea armata*) with stiff, fan-shaped, pale blue leaves and

the lady palm (*Rhapis excelsa*), which tolerates low light levels. Both are fairly hardy.

- *Gunnera manicata* (above centre): This magnificent beast, which has enormous scalloped leaves like a giant rhubarb, takes up a lot of space but creates an exotic feel. Grow it in boggy soil with a punctured plastic sack underneath.
- Plume poppy (*Macleaya cordata*): A tall plant that dies back to the ground each year. It has large, lobed leaves and plumes of tiny flowers.
- Castor oil plant (*Fatsia japonica*) (see page 79): With its big, glossy, evergreen leaves, this

plant will grow in dismal gloom and is as tough as old boots.

- Rice paper plant (*Tetrapanax papyrifer*): This sparsely branched shrub or small tree. has large, lobed leaves.
- Honey bush (*Melianthus major*): This has large, serrated, blue-green leaves. It should survive outdoors in a warm garden, but may die back to ground level in winter. If you take it indoors in a pot, it will be evergreen. It tolerates shade but prefers sun. Cut it back in spring if it gets straggly.
- Tree ferns: *Dicksonia antarctica* is the most hardy. Keep the trunk (actually a bundle of

roots) moist; pour a bucket of water over it every day in warm weather. Grow it somewhere cool, out of sun.

- Bamboos: Black bamboo (*Phyllostachys nigra*) has interesting blackish stems; golden bamboo (*Phyllostachys aurea*) has bright yellow canes. *Sasa veitchii* has large green leaves that wither around the edges, giving the appearance of a creamy stripe. Bamboos like lots of fertilizer and moist soil. Some are very invasive if not restrained by a pot, so watch out or they could take over your garden.

purple-leaved plants

- Purple sage (*Salvia officinalis* Purpurascens Group): Purple-flushed felty leaves make a low aromatic evergreen mound.
- Teinturier grape, purple vine (*Vitis vinifera* 'Purpurea'): Leaves open wine and turn deep purple. Grow in a sunny, sheltered spot. Unfortunately, its grapes are revolting.
- Purple New Zealand flax (*Phormium tenax* Purpureum Group): With its sword-like evergreen leaves, this dramatic plant is an eye-catcher.
- Coral flower (*Heuchera micrantha* var. *diversifolia* 'Palace Purple'): A low-growing

BUYING PLANTS

Before you buy, make sure your plant is healthy:

- Check that the plant has healthy-looking leaves: no yellowing, no brown patches, no wilting, no mildew, no holes where they've been eaten.
- Look underneath the pot to see whether roots are sticking out. If they are, the plant may be pot bound (its roots haven't been able to spread so they have gone around in a circle) and it won't grow well.
- Choose a well-shaped, balanced plant and check that no branches have been snapped off.

plant with sultry purple leaves. Or try 'Pewter Moon' for purple leaves with a silvery metallic patina.

- Purple smoke bush (*Cotinus coggygria* 'Royal Purple') (above left): A big shrub with neat, round, dark purple leaves that turn brilliant red in autumn and clouds of tiny summer flowers (hence its name). This plant is widely available; cut it back hard if it gets too big. *Cotinus* 'Grace' has bright claret-coloured leaves.
- Japanese maples (*Acer palmatum*) (above right): These are graceful mini-trees

with delicate leaves. There are masses of types, some green-leaved, some purple-leaved.
- Purple barberry (*Berberis thunbergii* f. atropurpurea): A prickly dense bush with little purple leaves that turn vermillion in autumn. There is also a dwarf version.

hedging plants
- Yew (*Taxus baccata*): A poisonous evergreen that is good for formal and traditional gardens in sun or shade; medium growing speed, medium to tall hedges.
- Box (*Buxus sempervirens*): Evergreen, good for formal

and traditional gardens in sun or shade; slow-growing, low to medium-height hedges. The dwarf variety ('Suffruticosa') could be used for miniature hedges.
- Hornbeam (*Carpinus betulus*) and beech (*Fagus sylvatica*): Deciduous, but as hedges these plants tend to hold their dead, russet leaves through the winter (and remain reasonably opaque); medium to very high hedges.
- Holly (*Ilex*): Evergreen; sun or shade; slow-growing.
- Privet (*Ligustrum* varieties): Evergreen, good in sun or shade; fast-growing (so

requires regular trimming); medium to high hedges, not particularly dense, so hedges can get gappy.
- Laurel (*Prunus laurocerasus*): Evergreen, large glossy leaves; good in town gardens in sun or shade; fairly fast-growing, medium to tall hedges.
- Portugal laurel (*Prunus lusitanica*): Evergreen, good in sun or shade; attractive contrast between red stalks and dark green leaves; fast-growing; medium to tall hedges.
- Lavender (*Lavendula* species): Evergreen, good in sun; scented and flowering; low, informal hedges.

- Rosemary (*Rosmarinus officinalis*): Evergreen, good in sun; aromatic, flowering and edible; low, informal hedges. 'Miss Jessopp's Upright' is less sprawling.
- Hedgehog rose (*Rosa rugosa*): Long-flowering, not evergreen; low to medium height. The 'Canary Bird' rose can also be lightly trimmed to make a loose, informal hedge.
- Shrubby honeysuckle (*Lonicera nitida*): Evergreen and fast-growing, so needs clipping twice a year to stay neat; sun or shade; low to medium height hedges.
- Japanese quince (*Chaenomeles speciosa*): This can be trimmed to form a tangled informal hedge. Flowers appear on the bare branches in winter and spring; sun or shade; low to medium height hedges.

multi-talented plants

In a small garden, it's a good idea to use plants that have more than one good feature. If you hunt carefully, you can find clever plants that offer pretty spring flowers and amazing autumn leaf colour, or colourful winter bark and superb summer foliage.

TREES

- Snowy mespilus (*Amelanchier lamarckii*): This has dainty white spring blossom, coppery young leaves, black fruits, gorgeous orange autumn leaves and a delicate, multi-stemmed habit.
- Tibetan cherry (*Prunus serrula*): Polished, rich copper bark, sparse white spring flowers on bare branches as the pretty tapered leaves emerge.
- Strawberry tree (*Arbutus unedo*): Rough, reddish bark, glossy evergreen leaves, pendent clusters of small white flowers and striking bright red spherical fruit.
- Crab apple (*Malus* 'Golden Hornet'): Bright green toothed leaves, pink buds open into white flowers and, later, profuse and long-lasting small golden apples.
- Chinese birch (*Betula albosinensis* var. *septentrionalis*): Warm orange-pink bark, dainty leaves, spring catkins and yellow autumn leaf colour.

SHRUBS

- *Rosa moyesii* 'Geranium': Graceful arching branches, simple red flowers in early summer, long-lasting hips in autumn and winter.
- Guelder rose (*Viburnum opulus* 'Compactum'): 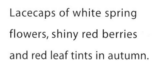 Lacecaps of white spring flowers, shiny red berries and red leaf tints in autumn.
- *Fothergilla major*: Fragrant white bottle-brush flowers on bare branches or, as the leaves unfold, glossy green leaves that turn a kaleidoscope of colours in autumn as they prepare to fall.
- Variegated dogwood (*Cornus alba* 'Elegantissima'): Lovely grey-green and white leaves that turn red and orange in autumn, striking dark red twigs in winter and white flowers in late spring.
- Witch hazel (*Hamamelis* x *intermedia* 'Diane'): Fragrant spidery red winter flowers on bare branches, bright green leaves that turn red, orange and yellow in autumn.
- *Ceratostigma willmottianum*: Deciduous shrub with blue flowers in late summer and autumn and mid-green leaves that turn red in autumn.

PERENNIALS AND BIENNIALS

When you're selecting smaller plants, find out what they'll look like when they're not flowering. If they'll be a big blot of tatty leaves (or bare soil) for most of the year, it may be better to give them a miss.

plants for hot spots

(See also easy herbs, pages 152–3, and silver and blue plants, page 64.)

- Broom (*Cytisus*): Shrubs that are easy to grow in hot, dry sites. Most get smothered in a mass of small yellow flowers and tolerate atmospheric pollution. Some varieties have outlandish two-tone flowers (look for 'Hollandia' which is cream and dark pink).

- Sun rose (*Cistus* x *purpureus*): Rounded shrub with aromatic sticky shoots and evergreen leaves that provide a good backdrop for the dark pink tissue-paper flowers.

- Rock rose (*Helianthemum*): Small sprawling, evergreen plants, often with greyish leaves and charming papery flowers from late spring to mid-summer. 'Fire Dragon' has orange-red flowers; 'Wisley Primrose' has pale yellow ones.

- Yarrow (*Achillea*): Flat horizontal heads of tiny flowers, these look great combined with vertical flower spikes (like *Salvia* x *superba* which has spikes of violet purple flowers). 'Coronation Gold' is rich yellow, 'Cerise Queen' is magenta pink.

- Red valerian (*Centranthus ruber*): Easy perennial with upright stems topped with rounded clusters of tiny dark crimson flowers throughout summer. It grows well on old stone walls or in cracks in paving. There are white and pink-flowered forms, too. It self-seeds readily so take care to deadhead it if you don't want it to pop up everywhere.

- Cape figwort (*Phygelius capensis*): Upright shrub with spikes of pendent, tubular, orange flowers in summer. The variety called 'Coccineus' has scarlet flowers.

- Stonecrop (*Sedum* 'Ruby Glow'): A low-growing perennial with purplish leaves (that disappear in winter) and ruby-red flowers in late summer and early autumn. Some (like *Sedum acre* and *Sedum spathulifolium*) make ground-covering mats with tiny rosettes of fleshy leaves.

- *Nerine bowdenii*: Easy bulbs to grow along the base of a sunny wall (in well-drained soil) for exotic pink flowers in autumn. Should come up year after year.

- Jerusalem sage (*Phlomis fruticosa*): Mound-forming evergreen shrub with felty, greyish leaves and golden yellow flowers in summer.

EDIBLE FLOWERS

Spice up your salads by adding a handful of flowers. Impress (or alarm) your guests by using flowers picked from your own garden. Use peppery orange, red or yellow nasturtiums (above), yellow or purple violas, vivid orange pot marigolds and sugary day lilies.

- Monkshood (*Aconitum*) (very poisonous) and day lilies (*Hemerocallis*): Both have attractive, fresh leaves that come up early in spring.

- Cranesbill (*Geranium* x *magnificum*): This has leaves that colour in autumn, and violet mid-summer flowers. Balkan cranesbill (*Geranium macrorrhizum*) has aromatic leaves that colour in autumn, and purple-pink early summer flowers.

- Lady's mantle (*Alchemilla mollis*) (above right): This has lovely scalloped leaves and long-lasting sprays of tiny lime-green flowers.

- Honesty (*Lunaria annua*): A biennial that bears spring flowers (either white or purple) followed by silvery semi-transparent disc-shaped seedheads that persist throughout winter (see page 145).

Nasturtiums, gazanias, pot marigolds, love-in-a-mist (*Nigella*), sweet peas, Cosmos Sonata Series, Californian poppies (*Eschscholzia*) and Osteospermums all provide easy flowers in sun.

plants with great green leaves

Leaves last longer than flowers, so make sure you have plenty of plants with beautiful leaves.

- Loquat (*Eriobotrya japonica*): Large evergreen shrub (or small tree) with handsome, glossy, ridged leaves. Its fragrant white flowers are a bonus. If this plant is really happy, it could even give you some edible fruit.
- Kohuhu (*Pittosporum tenuifolium*): Bushy evergreen shrub with shiny, wavy-edged green leaves borne on attractively contrasting blackish twigs. It has honey-scented flowers in late spring.
- Japanese maple (*Acer palmatum*): Small or tiny deciduous trees; many different types, some have delicate, finely dissected, filigree leaves, some have spiky, palmate leaves.
- Bear's breeches (*Acanthus spinosus*): A perennial with magnificent, large, jagged spiny leaves. Grows almost anywhere. It also has bold spikes of hooded flowers that dry to look good in winter. *Acanthus mollis* is less fierce-looking. Not evergreen.
- *Viburnum davidii*: Evergreen shrub that forms a neat dome. Each leaf is etched with three deep grooves. If you grow male and female plants together, you'll get bizarre metallic azure berries.
- Lady's mantle (*Alchemilla mollis*) (left): This small plant is a must-have; squeeze it in somewhere. Its delightful scalloped leaves trap rain and dew drops and look as though they're studded with diamonds. Not evergreen.
- Ferns, astilbes and hostas: All of these give a wide range of wonderful leaves and grow well in shade. Hostas are pure ambrosia to slugs and snails, so keep a vigilant lookout for the little monsters. Some hardy geraniums have very pretty lacy foliage (and charming flowers as a bonus).

golden plants

If you want more sun in your garden, fake it with golden plants. These are great for shady gardens where they glow in the gloom (in full sun, some golden-leaved plants get scorched, leaving them browned and sickly looking).

- Golden false acacia (*Robinia pseudoacacia* 'Frisia'): This fast-growing, show-stopping tree with fluorescent lime-green foliage, will provide a big splash of sun (if you've got the space). Sun or shade.
- Golden mock orange (*Philadelphus coronarius* 'Aureus'): Easy deciduous shrub bearing creamy summer flowers with an orangey scent. Grow in shade.
- Golden elder (*Sambucus racemosa* 'Plumosa Aurea'): A large, deciduous shrub. Cut it back viciously in early spring for fresh foliage (and to keep it controlled). Grow in shade.
- Golden shrubby honeysuckle (*Lonicera nitida* 'Baggesen's Gold'): Easy-to-grow evergreen shrub with arching branches bearing tiny leaves. It can be clipped to form a solid shape or low hedge. If it's planted somewhere sunny, the foliage may become unattractively bleached.
- At ground level, try Bowles' golden grass, golden hostas, golden marjoram and golden spotted dead nettle. Cover walls with golden hop and bright yellow 'Buttercup' ivy.

PLANTING BULBS

Plant bulbs so that they are covered by three times the depth of the bulb in soil (the base of the bulb should be four times the depth of the bulb below ground). Use a layer of drainage material in the base of the container or in the bottom of the planting hole and add grit or coarse sand to the soil for good drainage so the bulb doesn't rot. Plant daffodils and narcissi in early autumn. Plant tulips in late autumn. Bulbs generally look better planted in groups of six or more.

Note – for bulbs to flower properly the following year, you should feed them and let their leaves die back naturally (don't cut them off before they have started to turn yellow) so that the bulb can replenish its energies. This isn't necessary for bulbs you are going to replace (like many tulips, which won't flower well in the following year anyway).

easy bulbs

For extra flowers, plant drifts of bulbs in perennial beds and grass or squeeze them into your containers. Grow winter and early spring bulbs under deciduous shrubs for flowers when the shrub's branches are bare. When the bulbs are over and their foliage begins to die back, the shrub will come into leaf and hide the unattractive leaves. You can use bulbs in containers among permanent plants or add them to seasonal containers as you plant them up in autumn or spring. Pick them up in your local garden centre, or your supermarket may even stock some. Browse through mail-order catalogues for a wider choice.

- Snowdrops (*Galanthus*): Dainty, bell-shaped, white flowers; mid-winter onwards. Deadhead to prevent seeds from forming.
- Crocus: Diminutive flowers that give welcome early colour; look for white, yellow, pink or purple.
- Hyacinths (*Hyacinthus*): Lusciously scented plump spikes of flowers, commonly in white, pink and blue. After the first year of flowering the flower spikes will be smaller, but still very pretty.

- Grape hyacinths (*Muscari* species) (above): Easy bulbs that produce small spikes of tiny rounded flowers in late spring and early summer. Commonly dark blue but white and pale blue types can also be found. They look great on their own in small pots.
- Daffodils and narcissi (*Narcissus* varieties): There's a huge range of these lovely (and easy) flowers. Some are small and dainty, others are the well-known, exuberant yellow trumpets that herald spring. Some have a fabulous scent. Flowers range from white to yellow, some have a coloured 'eye' in the middle. Different varieties flower from winter to spring. Deadhead to prevent seed from forming.
- Tulips (*Tulipa*): Many tulips only flower well in their first year, so you'll need to replace them each year. This makes tulips an expensive option but, for the truly magnificent flowers, it's worth splashing out on enough for a pot or two. Look for frilly parrot tulips for old-world splendour or elegant lily-flowered tulips with their pointed petals and tapering blooms. Using a single type and colour in a pot is a stylish way to enjoy them.

long-flowering plants

In a small garden, grow some great performers that will flower prettily for weeks on end.

- *Erigeron karvinskianus* (above): A wonderful plant that makes sprawling mounds of foliage smothered with pink and white daisy flowers from spring to autumn. It spreads readily and is very happy planted in a wall or in paving.
- Perennial wallflower (*Erysimum* 'Bowles Mauve'): Bushy evergreen plant with mauve flowers virtually all year round. It gets leggy so replace it every couple of years.

- *Osteospermum*: Evergreen plants with funky daisy flowers from spring to autumn. Some have light-reflecting petals that make them almost luminous in the evening. Colours include white, yellow and pink-purple. Buy them in flower to be sure. Look for 'Whirligig', which has extraordinary spoon-shaped petals. They aren't very hardy but should survive outside in a city garden. Deadhead regularly and replace them if they get straggly. Grow them in a bright spot in well-drained soil; they tolerate erratic watering.

- Japanese anemones (*Anemone x hybrida*): Tolerant plants with lovely flowers from mid-summer into autumn.
- Stinking hellebore (*Helleborus foetidus*): Evergreen plant with persistent clusters of pale green flowers that last from winter to spring. Usually the flowers have a narrow margin, as if they have been dipped in dark red paint.
- Trailing abutilon (*Abutilon megapotamicum*): Evergreen or semi-evergreen shrub with dangling, red and yellow flowers over an incredibly long period (virtually all year). For a very gaudy look, there is a variegated type, with yellow-splashed leaves.
- Potato vine (*Solanum jasminoides*): Evergreen or semi-evergreen climber that flowers all summer and autumn. 'Album' has white flowers rather than the normal blue-white colour. It isn't very hardy, so plant it somewhere sheltered.
- Blue daisy (*Felicia amelloides*) (see page 150): Rounded bushy plant with dainty blue daisies from June to September in full sun. It tolerates partial shade, but don't plant it in soggy soil. Pinch back young shoots to keep it bushy.

- Mallow (*Lavatera*) (see page 16): This shrub flowers for a long time (throughout summer until the first autumn frosts). It is fast-growing and needs to be pruned hard each spring (cut it back to near ground level). For a change from the usual strong mauve-pink opt for pale pink 'Barnsley' instead.
- Horned violet (*Viola cornuta*): Charming plant that forms a sprawling mound of subtle white, bluish or pale purple flowers from spring to autumn. Grow in sun or partial shade in moist soil.
- Many summer bedding plants flower all summer long and on into autumn.

and for the lazy gardener ...

Grow weed-beating ground-cover plants and shrubs you don't have to prune.

WEED-BEATING GROUND-COVERERS

Use ground-cover plants so weeding becomes a distant memory (well, almost). The idea is simple – you grow a thick layer of desirable plants over bare soil to stop undesirable ones coming up (there's no room for them to grow). It's easy to achieve and a lush carpet of plants looks far better than areas of bare soil. Choose tough competitive plants, which will hog their space and keep everything else at bay. Watch out though: some ground-coverers rapidly spread, engulfing everything in their path, whether weed or not. Avoid these in a small space (particularly if you've got delicate treasures nearby).

Apart from low-growing ground-covers (listed below), some bushes, including most evergreens, act as their own ground-cover, preventing anything from growing beneath them. But weeds can grow (and any bare soil will be visible) under tall, airy or deciduous trees and shrubs. So plant shade-tolerant ground-coverers under them to suppress the weeds and hide any bare soil. For the effect of dappled sunlight in a dark corner, use a ground-cover plant with white or yellow-splashed (variegated) leaves. Always use plenty of plants so they will quickly knit together to form a carpet. Most bulbs will manage to push up and flower through ground-cover planting, so plant some at the same time for extra flowers (see easy bulbs, page 148).

FOR SHADY PLACES

- Dead nettle (*Lamium maculatum*): Low carpets of patterned leaves. 'White Nancy' has lovely silver-washed foliage.
- Bugle (*Ajuga reptans*): Neat mats of evergreen foliage. 'Burgundy Glow' has deep-red suffused leaves.
- *Pachysandra terminalis*: Very tough, will even grow beneath trees and shrubs in dry shade.
- Periwinkle (use *Vinca minor* not *Vinca major* which is very invasive): Evergreen, very tough, with pretty flowers.
- Bishop's mitre (*Epimedium* x *perralchicum*): Glossy green leaves, bronze when young.
- Mind-your-own-business (*Soleirolia soleirolii*): Creeps over shaded areas (including paving) making mounds of lovely mossy foliage.

FOR SUNNY PLACES

- Catmint (catnip) (*Nepeta* 'Six Hills Giant'): Lavender-blue flowers and aromatic grey leaves. Cut back after flowering for fresh leaves.
- Lambs' ears (*Stachys byzantina*): Rosettes of extremely felty grey leaves. Woolly spikes of pink-purple flowers all summer.

- Cranesbill (*Geranium dalmaticum*): Lacy leaves and clear pink flowers in summer.
- Creeping thyme (*Thymus serpyllum*): Mats of tiny evergreen aromatic leaves and white or pink flowers.

ALMOST ANYWHERE

- Lady's mantle (*Alchemilla mollis*): Pretty scalloped leaves topped with frothy greenish flowers.
- Elephant's ears (*Bergenia*): Huge round evergreen leaves.
- Balkan cranesbill (*Geranium macrorrhizum*): Semi-evergreen aromatic leaves.

- London pride (*Saxifraga* x *urbium*): Mat of evergreen leaves and fluffy pink flowers.
- Mrs Robb's bonnet (*Euphorbia amygdaloides* var. *robbiae*): Upright spikes of leathery evergreen leaves. It tolerates virtually any conditions including dry shade.
- Ivy (*Hedera*): Many make excellent ground-cover. Use a small one in a small space.

no-prune shrubs

If your attitude is 'love them and leave them' once you've put a plant in the ground, you'd better invest in a few easy shrubs. Unlike many deciduous shrubs, most evergreens don't need annual pruning to look good. Only cut them back (in late winter or early spring when they are dormant) if they get too unruly.

- Easy evergreen shrubs include laurustinus (*Viburnum tinus*), Mexican orange blossom (*Choisya ternata*), spindle (*Euonymus fortunei*), castor oil plant (*Fatsia japonica*) (right), *Mahonia japonica, Mahonia aquifolium,* skimmias, camellias (must have acid soil) and Christmas box (*Sarcococca*). Holly (*Ilex*) is slow-growing but it will eventually get big without requiring pruning.

- Daphnes: These hate being pruned so hold back with the secateurs (clippers). Many are richly fragrant, and most are compact and ideal for a small garden. Look for *Daphne bholua* (late winter flowers), *Daphne* x *burkwoodii* (late spring flowers) and *Daphne odora* (mid-winter to early spring flowers).

- Dwarf lilac (*Syringa*): Don't bother with a large lilac in a small garden; they look utterly dull for most of the year. Go for a dwarf variety for the delicious scent and pretty flowers. Best

of all, they don't need pruning. *Syringa meyeri* var. *spontanea* 'Palibin' has purple-pink flowers in late spring.

- Hardy hibiscus (*Hibiscus syriacus*): No pruning required. These are medium-sized deciduous shrubs with exotic trumpet-shaped flowers from late summer to mid-autumn. 'Blue Bird' is commonly available and has bright blue flowers. Look for 'Red Heart', which has white flowers with a dark red centre, and 'Diana', which has large white flowers.

atmospheric pollution-tolerant plants

If you're gardening in a smoggy environment, sickly plants will make it seem even worse. Use resilient specimens that will look good despite unfavourable conditions. The following all tolerate atmospheric pollution:

TREES

Mop-head acacia (*Robinia pseudoacacia* 'Umbraculifera'), great white cherry (*Prunus* 'Taihaku'), Japanese cherry (*Prunus* 'Amanogawa'), weeping silver pear (*Pyrus salicifolia* 'Pendula'), wild cherry (*Prunus avium* 'Plena'), golden Indian bean tree (*Catalpa bignonioides* 'Aurea'), black mulberry (*Morus nigra*), whitebeam (*Sorbus aria* 'Lutescens'), strawberry tree (*Arbutus unedo*), crab apples (*Malus*), laburnum (poisonous), hawthorns (*Cratageus*), hollies (*Ilex*) and magnolias.

SHRUBS

Hebes, broom (*Cytisus*), mock orange (*Philadelphus*), tamarisk (*Tamarix tetrandra*), barberry (*Berberis thunbergii*), hedgehog roses (*Rosa rugosa*), New Zealand flax (*Phormium*), sun roses (*Cistus* x *purpureus*), elders (*Sambucus*), hardy hybrid rhododendrons, Japanese quince (*Chaenomeles*), camellias, box, privet, *Elaeagnus* x *ebbingei*, castor oil plant, dog-wood (*Cornus alba*), laurustinus, Californian lilac (*Ceanothus*), Iceberg rose, mahonias, spindle (*Euonymus fortunei*), skimmias, forsythia, Christmas box (*Sarcococca*) and hydrangeas.

CLIMBERS

Jasmine (*Jasminum officinale*), Virginia creeper (*Parthenocissus quinquefolia*), climbing hydrangea (*Hydrangea petiolaris*), Chinese Virginia creeper (*Parthenocissus henryana*), ivies and Boston ivy (*Parthenocissus tricuspidata*).

GRUBBY LEAVES

In a polluted city, plants soon get a layer of grime on their leaves, making it harder for them to photosynthesize (quite apart from giving the plant a shabby look). Use a damp cloth to wipe the leaves clean. You could finish off with a leaf-shine spray.

groovy grasses

With their long-lasting allure, grasses are valuable in a limited space. They bring dynamism, texture and a delightful rustling sound to the garden. Plant huge swathes in the border for a billowing sea or use a striking single specimen in a container.

- Eulalia grass (*Miscanthus sinensis*): Tall grass with feathery plumes that sway over the leaves. 'Silberfeder' has good silky plumes; 'Zebrinus' has outlandish, cream-banded leaves.
- Feathertop (*Pennisetum villosum*): Often grown as an annual, this adorable grass has tactile flower heads like fluffy rabbit's tails.
- Blue oat grass (*Helictotrichon sempervirens*): This grass produces tufts of greyish-blue leaves. It will tolerate dry soil and is evergreen.
- Feather reed grass (*Calamagrostis* x *acutiflora* 'Karl Foerster'): Tall, erect grass with airy pinkish flower heads. After the leaves have died, the skeleton remains to haunt the garden in winter (don't cut it back if you like the effect).
- Bronze sedge (*Carex comans* bronze): Evergreen clumps of bronzed leaves.
- Bowles' golden sedge (*Carex hachijoensis* 'Evergold'): Evergreen sedge that forms a striking hummock of striped green and bright yellow leaves.
- Blue fescue (*Festuca glauca*): Small spiky tussocks of glaucous foliage that gradually turn a startling bright blue as the weather gets sunnier. The type called 'Blaufuchs' has the bluest leaves. It's evergreen.
- *Hakonechloa macra* 'Aureola': Gracefully arching grass with fascinating striped leaves that merit close inspection.
- Pheasant's tail grass (*Stipa arundinacea*): Evergreen, medium-sized arching grass with orange-brown streaked leaves that turn fully orange-brown in winter.
- Giant feather grass (*Stipa gigantea*): Ethereal flower heads held high above the leaves on slim stems in summer. Evergreen or semi-evergreen.
- Feather grass (*Stipa tenuissima*): Medium-sized grass with extraordinary downy clumps of ultra-fine leaves and flower heads that sway enchantingly in the slightest breeze. Deciduous, but the dried dead leaves look good, too.

easy herbs

Most herbs love lots of sun and gritty, well-drained soil. Grow them in a hot spot, add plenty of drainage material when you plant them, and water sparingly (unless otherwise indicated).

- Thyme (*Thymus* species): Low-growing and evergreen with pink flowers in spring. Trim back after flowering to stop it getting straggly. Dwarf thymes look great in paving.
- Rosemary (*Rosmarinus officinalis*): Bushy evergreen shrub that gets quite big. It has pungently aromatic foliage and a mass of small blue flowers in spring.
- Chives (*Allium schoenoprasum*): Tolerant plant with stringy leaves and pink pompom

flowers in June and July. The leaves die down in winter to re-emerge in spring. Water through the summer to keep a good supply of leaves.

- Basil (*Ocimum basilicum*): More tricky and frost sensitive, but so delicious it's worth the effort. Sow seed on a bright window sill indoors in spring. Water sparingly and only in the morning. Transplant the seedlings into small pots (don't put them outside until all risk of frost has passed). Plant them in a sheltered corner in light soil with plenty of grit and keep the soil moist.

- Mint (*Mentha* species): It is best to grow mint in a pot as it can quickly romp through a flower bed. Choose from a range of mints with different scents and foliage. Mint likes some shade and moist soil.

- Bay (*Laurus nobilis*): Aromatic evergreen tree or bush that thrives in a sheltered spot. Can be clipped into a standard (lollipop shape).

- Sage (*Salvia officinalis*): Evergreen bush with lovely felted leaves that form a low mound. Choose between green, purple, green and yellow or 'Tricolor'.

- Marjoram (*Origanum vulgare*): Makes low hummocks of foliage. Look for the golden type, too. Give it a trim after flowering to keep it bushy.

- Coriander (*Coriandrum sativum*): An annual that should be grown from seed each year. Sow seed in pots or in the ground in a sunny position from early spring onwards. Keep sowing little patches for a fresh supply.

- Parsley (*Petroselinum crispum*): Grow it fresh from seed each year. Plant it in the ground or in pots in spring and summer (soak the seeds overnight to get them to germinate). Use flat-leaved or crisped-leaved types. It likes moist soil.

plants to grow in grass

Clear areas in a lawn and plant bulbs or perennials. Water them regularly until they get going, and let the bulb leaves turn yellow before mowing the grass.

- Snake's head fritillaries (*Fritillaria meleagris*), ox-eye daisies (*Leucanthemum vulgare*), meadow cranesbill (*Geranium pratense*), primroses (*Primula vulgaris*), snowdrops, crocus and dwarf narcissus.

GLOSSARY

Acid soil – soil with a low pH (you can buy kits to test the pH). Some plants need acid (or neutral) soil to grow properly (like rhododendrons). If your soil isn't acid, grow them in pots using ericaceous compost (potting soil).

Alkaline soil – soil with a high pH. Not suitable for plants like camellias and rhododendrons, but certain plants like it (including most ornamental cherries).

Annuals – plants that only live for one growing season; they usually die in winter when the frosts arrive.

Bare-rooted plants – plants with roots that are not in a container or soil. These can be bought in winter when the plant isn't growing. Plant them immediately and they should start growing happily in spring.

Bedding plant – plant that is planted with many others for a temporary display. The Victorians started the craze for multicoloured mass plantings.

Biennials – plants that live for two years, flowering the second year.

Bonsai – a way of making dwarf trees and shrubs (from plants that would naturally be larger) by special techniques that include pruning roots and shoots and training branches and stems.

Cobblestones – smooth, water-worn, rounded stones (like large pebbles).

Cultivar – a cultivated (man-made) variety of a plant. The name of the cultivar is given in inverted commas; for example, *Galanthus nivalis* is the wild snowdrop, whereas *G. nivalis* 'Flore Pleno' is a cultivated variety with double flowers and *G. nivalis* 'Peg Sharples' is another type, probably bred by Mr or Mrs Sharples.

Cutting – a piece of a plant (usually a stem or leaf) that is removed and used to make a new plant (this is called propagation).

Dead-head – to remove faded flowers before seeds develop to promote further flowering or prevent the plant from self-seeding.

Deciduous – describes a woody plant (tree or shrub) that drops its leaves in autumn and regrows them in spring.

Double flower – flower with more than one layer of petals.

Ericaceous compost – special acid compost (potting soil) for acid soil-loving plants. You can buy it at any good garden centre.

Evergreen – a plant that doesn't drop all its leaves in autumn (it loses older leaves regularly throughout the year) and has foliage all year round.

Geo-textile membrane – a fabric that is porous to water but weeds can't grow through it. Lay it over the soil to minimize weeding (disguise it with gravel, cobbles or other mulch). Available at any good garden centre.

Ground-cover plants – low-growing plants that spread to form a blanket over the soil and suppress weeds.

Hardy – describes a plant that won't be killed by frost and that should survive the winter outside in temperate climates.

Herbaceous – describes a plant which dies back to ground level in autumn and re-emerges in spring.

Invasive plant – certain plants (for example mint and some bamboos) are rampant growers and won't stay where you plant them; they may smother anything nearby and it could be wise to grow them in a container (which you could bury in the soil).

Mortar – smooth mixture of cement, sand and water for fixing bricks or stones in place. Old-fashioned mortar contained lime instead of cement.

Mulch – anything used to cover the soil to keep it moist and suppress weeds. Try gravel, stone chippings, bark chips or even lawn clippings. Organic mulches break down to enrich the soil with nutrients.

Neutral soil – soil with a pH value of 7; it is neither acid nor alkaline.

Perennials – plants that live for more than two years.

Poor soil – soil containing low levels of nutrients/plant food.

Rich soil – soil containing lots of nutrients/plant food.

Self-clinging climber – climbing plant that grows without support (like wires or trellis). It can simply sticks onto a wall or fence. Some have little suckers, others have aerial roots.

Shrub – a bush (woody plant, smaller than a tree; usually its main stem branches at or near ground level).

Single flower – flower with one layer of petals.

Soil pH test kit – kit to determine whether your soil is acid, neutral or alkaline; you should be able to buy one at any good garden centre.

Standards – lollipop-shaped plants with a long bare stem topped by a mop of bushy leaves and branches. Some plants can be pruned, clipped and trained to form standards; look for pre-trained roses, fuchsias, hollies, rosemary, marguerites (margaritas) (*Argyranthemum frutescens*), the Kilmarnock willow, citrus trees, common hydrangeas (*Hydrangea macrophylla*), gooseberries and laurustinus (*Viburnum tinus*).

Succulent plant – plant with thick fleshy leaves and stems. Usually evergreen. Often frost tender.

Tender or frost tender – describes a plant that won't (or may not) survive the winter outside in temperate climates; frost will kill it, so take it indoors or into a frost-free greenhouse for protection.

Trailing plant – plant with floppy stems that hang down.

Trompe l'oeil – French phrase for a painting or decoration designed to create an illusion (literally, trick the eye).

Variegated – variegated leaves have yellow (golden variegated) or white/cream (silver variegated) patterns on them.

DIRECTORY

UK

Buildings, Marquees & Awnings

Belle Tents
Owl's Gate, Davidstow, Camelford, Cornwall PL32 9XY
Tel/Fax: 01840 261556
Web: www.belletents.com
Custom-made marquees.

The Children's Cottage Co.
The Sanctuary, Shobrooke, Crediton, Devon EX17 1BG
Tel: 01363 772061
Fax: 01363 777868
High-quality wooden playhouses made to look like thatched or tiled cottages. Also, a wooden castle complete with shuttered windows and battlements.

The Cutting Edge Collection
Heatherhurst Lodge, Deepcut, Surrey GU16 6RL
Tel/fax: 01252 835735
Email: cemlodge@aol.com
Web: www.cutting-edge.gb.com
Traditional summerhouses, gazebos and arbours. Also urns, ornamental leadware, water features, decorative plaques and trelliswork.

Live in Art Ltd
Unit 12 Park Farm Buildings, Cranfield Road, Woburn Sands, Milton Keynes MK17 8UR
Tel: 01908 281556
Fax: 01908 584886
Email: paulgoldie@alfa-retreat.co.uk
Web: www.alfa-retreat.co.uk
The Alfa Retreat – a hexagonal building made from glass-reinforced plastic. Expensive but unusual and modern.

Mini Marquee Co.
20 Bradmore Park Road, London W6 0DF
Tel: 020 8741 2777
Fax: 020 8741 2888
Email: info@minimarquee.co.uk
Tents and marquees.

Tidmarsh and Sons
32 Hyde Way, Welwyn Garden City, Hertfordshire AL7 3AW
Tel: 01707 886226
Fax: 01707 886227
Email: blinds@tidmarsh.co.uk
Manual and electric awnings. Free measuring service within the M25 area. Installation nationwide.

Containers

Barbary Pots
45 Fernshaw Road, London SW10 0TN
Tel: 020 7352 1053
Fax: 020 7351 5504
Web: www.barbarypots.co.uk
Handmade Morroccan terracotta pots, some very large. London stockists or deliver nationwide. Can export.

Capital Garden Products
Gibbs Reed Barn, Pashley Road, Tichurst, East Sussex TN5 7HE
Tel: 01580 201092
Fax: 01580 201093
Email: sales@capital-garden.com
High-quality fibreglass containers, pond and wall fountains, wall plaques, pedestals and columns. Also aluminium, steel and canvas garden furniture. Mail order and export worldwide. Telephone for a free catalogue.

Patio Garden Centre
100 Tooting Bec Road, London SW17 8BG
Tel: 020 8672 2251
Hand-thrown terracotta pots from Italy, Crete and France, plus a range of plants, including herbs and Mediterranean plants.

Prêt-à-Pot
6A Cow Lane, Sidlesham, Chichester, West Sussex PO20 7LN
Tel: 01243 641928
Fax: 01243 641945
Email: info@pret-a-pot.com
Web: www.pret-a-pot.com
Beautiful glazed terracotta and galvanized steel pots (as seen in this book); straight-sided Long Toms a speciality.

Whichford Pottery
Whichford, Nr Shipston on Stour, Warwickshire CV36 5PG
Tel: 01608 684416
Fax: 01608 684833
Email: whichford_pottery@ compuserve.com
Web: www.whichfordpottery.com
High-quality handmade terracotta pieces, including pots, fountains, wall plaques, chickens and finials. Mail order, export or visit the pottery in person. Catalogue available.

Fences & Screens

English Hurdle Co.
Curload, Stoke St Gregory, Taunton, Somerset TA3 6JD
Tel: 01823 698418
Fax: 01823 698859
Email: hurdle@enterprise.net
Web: www.hurdle.co.uk
Handmade willow products. Willow fencing panels (hurdles), also willow arches, arbours, seats and plant supports.

Jungle Giants
Plough Farm, Wigmore, Herefordshire HR6 9UW
Tel: 01568 770708
Fax: 01568 770383
Bamboo poles, screens, fencing and gates. Also bamboo plants. Mail order and export.

Outdoor Interiors Ltd
PO Box 40, Woking, Surrey GU22 7YU
Tel: 01483 727888
Fax: 01483 727828
Email: info@outdoor-interiors.co.uk
Web: www.outdoor-interiors.co.uk

Pressure-impregnated softwood fences, trelliswork and screens. Also arches and pergolas. Supply nationwide. No fitting but can recommend installers nationwide. Telephone for a free catalogue. Mail or telephone order.

Stuart Garden Architecture
Burrow Hill Farm, Wiveliscombe, Somerset TA4 2RN
Tel: 01984 667458
Fax: 01984 667455
Email: trellis@stuartgarden.com
Web: www.stuartgarden.com
Trelliswork, planters, garden buildings, gazebos, pergolas, arbours, gates, bridges and seating. All products made in wood, mainly iroko. Telephone for a free brochure. Delivery nationwide.

Thatching Advisory Services
Faircross Offices, Stratfield Saye, Reading, Berkshire RG7 2BT
Tel: 01256 880828
Split bamboo, heather and peeled reed screening, reed and willow panels and bamboo fencing. Also, thatch tiles and umbrellas.

Flooring

Addagrip Surface Treatments
Bird-in-Eye Hill, Uckfield, East Sussex TN22 5HA
Tel: 01825 761333
Fax: 01825 768566
Email: roger@addagrip.co.uk
Web: www.addagrip.co.uk
Resin-bonded cobblestones, shingle, gravel and sand. Telephone for approved contractors and suppliers.

Bradstone Home and Garden Landscaping,
Hullard Ward, Ashbourne, Derbyshire DE6 3ET
Tel: 0800 975 9828
Web: www.bradstone.com
Natural and reconstituted stone slabs, blocks, cobblestones, aggregates, pots, planters and walling. Supply nationwide.

Civil Engineering Developments
728 London Road, West Thurrock, Grays, Essex RM20 3LU
Tel: 01708 867237
Fax: 01708 867230
Email: sales@ced.ltd.uk
Web: www.ced.ltd.uk
All natural stone including slabs, boulders, setts, cobblestones, pebbles, mosaic, aggregates. Supply nationwide.

Clever Decks
512 Beech Lane, Browns Hill, Gloucestershire GL6 8AJ
Tel: 01453 885903
Fax: 01453 885253
Email: jamesshowers@ sacredgardens.co.uk
Unusually shaped (curving, organic) decks in oak, cedar or pressure-treated softwood. Also a commissioning service for ornamental features, including mosaic, sculpture, water features, gates, stained glass and plant sculpture.

Edgar Udny & Co.
314 Balham High Road,
London SW17 7AA
Tel: 020 8767 8181
The UK's largest stockist of mosaic. Mail order available.

Ibstock Building Products
Leicester Road, Ibstock,
Leicestershire LE67 6HS
Tel: 01530 261999
Fax: 01530 257457
Web: www.ibstock.co.uk
Handmade and machined bricks, engineering bricks, ceramic tiles. Also terracotta, faience and cast-stone columns, balustrades, finials and urns.

Leisuredeck Ltd
311 Marsh Road, Leagrave, Luton,
Bedfordshire LU3 2RZ
Tel: 01582 563080
Fax: 01582 578384
Email: enquiry@leisuredeck.co.uk
Web: www.leisuredeck.co.uk
Western red cedar decking. Designed individually for each home. Estimates and work nationwide.

Marshalls
Southowram, Halifax,
West Yorkshire HX3 9SY
Tel: 01422 306000
Fax: 01422 330185
Web: www.marshalls.co.uk
Wide range of paving and walling materials. Natural stone slabs, setts, reproduction stone slabs and pavers. Telephone the brochure hotline on 01422 306090 for a catalogue.

Silverland Stone
Holloway Hill, Chertsey,
Surrey KT16 0AE
Tel: 01932 569277
Fax: 01932 563558
Email: gskilbeck@btinternet.com
All types of natural stone plus reclaimed materials and man-made paving and walling. Visit is preferable, brochure available on request.

Stonemarket
Old Gravel Quarry, Oxford Road, Ryton on Dunsmore, Warwickshire CV8 3EJ
Tel: 024 76305530
Fax: 024 76303397
Natural stone and good reproduction stone paving. Telephone for a brochure and information on stockists.

Terram Ltd
Mamhilad, Pontypool, Gwent NP4 0YR
Tel: 01495 757722
Fax: 01495 762383
Geo-textile membrane. Stockists nationwide.

Tower Ceramics
91 Parkway, London NW1 7PP
Tel: 0207 485 7192
Fax: 020 7267 9571
Web: www.soft.net.uk/parry/tower
Importers of unglazed Italian porcelain and slate tiles suitable for garden use. Also English quarry tiles. Range of colours available. Visit the showroom.

Windmill Aggregates
Windmill Works, Aythorpe Roding,
Great Dunmow, Essex CM6 1PQ
Tel: 01279 876987 or 01785 661018
Fax: 01279 876959 or 01785 665929
Email: sales@specialistaggregates.co.uk
Web: www.specialistaggregates.co.uk
All types of natural and glass gravel including coloured. Also crushed cds (very sparkly), crushed shell, crushed slate, metaleis pea gravel (including gold, silver, copper, burgundy and emerald). Mail order service or telephone for distributors including garden centres.

The York Handmade Brick Co.
Forest Lane, Alne,
North Yorkshire YO61 1TU
Tel: 01347 838881
Fax: 01347 838885
Email: sales@yorkhandmade.co.uk
Web: www.yorkhandmade.co.uk
Handmade bricks, pavers and terracotta floor tiles. Also, special patterned bricks for edging. Telephone for a brochure. Export worldwide.

Furniture, Accessories & Tools

Accademia Antiques
643c Fulham Road, London SW6 5PU
Tel: 020 7736 7088
Chandeliers and furniture.

Appley Hoare Antiques
30 Pimlico Road, London SW1W 8LJ
Tel: 020 7730 7070
Antiques.

Aria
295–6 Upper Street, London N1 2TU
Tel: 020 7704 1999
Fax: 020 7704 6333
Web: www.aria-shop.co.uk
Contemporary furniture and accessories.

Avant Garden
The Studio, 3 Dartmouth P.ace,
London W4 2RH
Tel: 020 8747 1794
Fax: 020 8994 0793
Email: sales@avantgarden.co.uk
Web: www.avantgarden.co.uk
Garden ornaments, including zinc planters, plant supports, topiary frames, wrought iron and wirework. Mail order or visit by appointment. Telephone for a catalogue.

Ou Baholyodin
First Floor, 12 Greatorex Street,
London E1 5NF
Tel: 020 7426 0666
Furniture and accessories.

Burgon & Ball Ltd
La Planta Works, Holme Lane,
Sheffield S6 2JY
Tel: 0114 233 8262
Fax: 0114 285 2518
Email: heather@burgonball.freeserve.co.uk
High-quality tools. Also topiary frames. Mail order only, phone for a catalogue.

Dominic Capon
Unit 9, Imperial Studios, Imperial Road, London SW6 2AG
Tel: 020 7736 3060
Accessories from India and Vietnam.

Conran Shop
Michelin House, 81 Fulham Road,
London SW3 6RD
Tel: 020 7589 7401
Fax: 020 7823 7015
Web: www.conran.com
Garden accessories and furniture.

Decordence
126 Talbot Road, London W11 1JA
Tel: 020 7792 4122
Furniture and accessories.

Jacqueline Edge
1 Courtnell Street, London W2 5BU
Tel: 020 7229 1172
Fax: 020 7727 4651
Email: info@jacquelineedge.com
Web: www.jacquelineedge.com
Garden ornaments, including terracotta pots and columns, loungers, Burmese barbecues, orchid boxes and bamboo deckchairs. Mail order from Website.

English Gardenwares
Tyrone House, Norton, Chichester,
West Sussex PO20 6NH
Tel/Fax: 01243 543 804
Terracotta garden chimineas (camp fires). Nationwide delivery.

Gaze Burvill
Newtonwood Workshop, Newton Valence, Alton, Hampshire GU34 3EW
Tel: 01420 587467
Fax: 01420 587354
Email: info@gazeburvill.com
Web: www.gazeburvill.com
High-quality contemporary furniture (particularly fabulous sun loungers). Mail order, export to USA, work to commission. Telephone for a brochure.

Gloss Ltd
274 Portobello Road, London W10 5TE
Tel: 020 8960 4146
e-mail: pascale@glossltd.u-net.com
Designers of soft-furnishings. Specialists in suede and leather. Mail order or view by appointment.

Graham & Green
4, 7 & 10 Elgin Crescent,
London W11 2JA
Tel: 020 7727 4594
Fax: 020 7229 9717
Web: www.graham&green.co.uk
Garden furnishings, ceramics and kitchenware. Mail order.

Habitat
196 Tottenham Court Road,
London W1P 9LD
Tel: 020 7631 3880
Fax: 020 7255 6043
Web: www.habitat.net
Garden furniture and accessories (in stock in spring and summer), fabrics, soft furnishings and lighting. Telephone 0845 601 0740 for your local store.

Hammock Gallery
42 Vanston Place, London SW6 1AX
Tel: 020 7610 1992
Fax: 020 7610 1991
Web: www.hammock-gallery.com
Hammocks, frames and ropes.

IKEA
2 Drury Way, North Circular Road,
London NW10 0TH
Tel: 020 8208 5600
Web: www.ikea.com
Phone 020 8233 2300 for stores nationwide. Furniture, seasonal gardening accessories and plants.

Cath Kidston
8 Clarendon Cross, London W11 4AP
Tel: 020 7221 4000
Web: www.cathkidston.co.uk
Vintage and new floral fabrics, furniture and accessories. Mail order.

Lister Lutyens
Hammonds Drive, Eastbourne,
East Sussex BN23 6PW
Tel: 01323 431177
Fax: 01323 639314
Email: sales@lister-lutyens.co.uk
Web: www.lister-lutyens.co.uk
High-quality teak garden furniture. Stockists nationwide.

Malabar
31–3 South Bank Business Centre,
London SW8 5BL
Tel: 020 7501 4220
Visit the showroom to see their range of Indian silks and natural cottons in stripes, checks and plains, or call for stockists.

Marks and Spencer
458 Oxford Street, London W1N 0AP
Tel: 020 7935 7954
Fax: 020 7486 5379
Web: www.marksandspencer.com
Most stores sell gardening products, including plant containers, indoor and outdoor plants, seeds and bulbs. Phone 020 7935 4422 for details.

Mark Maynard Antiques
651 Fulham Road.London SW6 5BU
Tel: 020 7731 3533
Antiques.

Marston & Langinger
192 Ebury Street. London SW1W 8UP
Tel: 020 7823 6829
Web: www.marsten-and-langinger.com
Furnishings and accessories for conservatories and garden rooms.

Milio Interiors
170 Westbourne Grove,
London W11 2RW
Tel: 020 7229 8200
Web: www.miliointeriors.com
Furniture and accessories.

Minh Mang
182 Battersea Park Road,
London SW11 4ND
Tel: 020 7498 3233
Email: minhmang@lineone.net
Vietnamese and Cambodian silks.

Mint
70 Wigmore Street, London W1H 9DL
Tel: 020 7224 4406
Home accessories.

The Modern Garden Co.
Hill Pasture, Broxted, Great Dunmow
Essex CM6 2BZ
Tel/Fax: 01279 851900
Email: Info@moderngarden.co.uk
Web: www.moderngarden.co.uk
Modern garden furniture in plastic, steel, aluminium, concrete and contemporary fabrics. Telephone for a free catalogue.

Jane Morris Interiors
641 Fulham Road, London SW6 5PU
Tel: 020 7610 6878
French antiques.

Nom
150 Walton Street, London SW3 2JJ
Tel: 020 7584 4158
Lacquerware, textiles and ceramics.

Pepper-Mint
5 Albemarle Way, London EC1V 4JB
Tel: 020 7490 3033
Web: www.pepper-mint.com
Stacking cubes.

Rachel Reynolds
The Shed, 121 Central Hill,
London SE19 1BY
Tel: 020 8240 9696
Email: rreynolds@theshedstudios.com
Web: www.the shedstudios.com
Modern garden furniture.

The Rug Company
124 Holland Park Avenue,
London W11 4UE
Tel: 020 7229 5148
Web: www.rugcompany.co.uk
Rugs. Mail order. Call 020 7467 0690 for a catalogue.

Eyr Saunders
7 Wensley Road, Grangefield,
Stockton-on-tees, TS18 4JQ
Tel: 01647 614243
Designer-maker.

Scientific Wire Co.
18 Raven Road, London E18 1HW
Tel: 020 8505 0002
Fax: 020 8559 1114
Email: wire@enterprise.net
Web: www.wires.co.uk
Range of wire including enamelled. Mail order available. Telephone for a list of products.

Tan Rokka
123 Regents Park Road,
London NW1 8BE
Tel: 020 7722 3999
Eastern furniture and accessories. Mail order.

Tobias & the Angel
66 White Hart Lane,
London SW13 0PZ
Tel: 020 8296 0058
Antiques.

Virginia Antiques
98 Portland Road, London W11 4LQ
Tel: 020 7727 9908
Antiques.

Garden Builders/Contractors

Ginkgo Landscapes
71B Tennyson Street, London SW8 3SU
Tel: 020 7498 2021
Fax: 020 7498 4695
Email: ToGinkgo@aol.com
Design and build.

Townscapes Landscape Contractors
30A Pimlico Road, London SW1 8LJ
Tel: 020 7730 7317 or 7730 4061
Fax: 020 7730 0480
Email: petergarland@townscapes.com
Design, build, maintain. London only.

Garden Designers

Rob Brewster
London
Tel: 020 7498 5690
Email: rwbrewster@yahoo.co.uk
Design and build small town gardens.

Rose Dale
London
Tel/Fax: 0207 727 2018
Email: rosedaledesign@hotmail.com
Design for your outdoor living space.

Alison Jenkins
London
Tel: 020 72744672 or 07956 267173
Email: alison@allium.freeserve.co.uk
Small urban spaces. Architectural planting.

Ross Palmer
London
Tel: 020 7684 9620
Fax: 020 7684 9621
Email: ross@palmergardens.com
Large commissions. International work.

Lee Pilkington
Norfolk
Tel: 01953 498356
Fax: 01953 498257
Email: l.pilkington@netcom.co.uk
Traditional and country gardens.

John Tordoff
London
Tel: 020 7254 5622
Email: jtordoff@tesco.net
Specializes in small town gardens.

Woodhams Landscape
Unit 3 McKay Trading Estate, Kensal Road, London W10 5BZ
Tel: 020 8964 9818
Fax: 020 8964 9848
Web: www.woodhams.co.uk
Large and small commissions.

Lighting & Irrigation

Indian Ocean
155–63 Balham Hill, London SW12 9DJ
Tel: 020 8675 4808

Fax: 020 8675 4652
Email: sales@indian-ocean.co.uk
Web: www.Indian-ocean.co.uk
Exterior lighting in wood, granite, copper and stainless steel. Large range of wooden garden furniture. Phone for a catalogue.

Leaky Pipe Systems Ltd
Frith Farm, Dean Street, Maidstone, Kent ME15 0PR
Tel: 01622 746495
Fax: 01622 745118
Email: sales@leakypipe.co.uk
Web: www.leakypipe.co.uk
Dripper systems for containers or porous hose systems for the garden.

Lighting for Landscapes
70 New Wokingham Road, Crowthorne, Berkshire RG45 6JJ
Tel: 01344 775232
Fax: 01344 775296
Email: john@-lightingforlandscapes.co.uk
Web:www.lightingforlandscapes.co.uk
Design, supply and installation of lighting in copper, stainless steel, brass and bronze. Minimum cost £1,000.

Outdoor Lighting Supplies (OLS)
Surrey Business Park, Weston Road, Epsom, Surrey KT17 1JG
Tel: 01372 848818
Fax: 01372 848801
Email: info@ols.co.uk
Web: www.louis-poulsen.com
Design consultation and supply of garden lighting. Phone for a brochure. No minimum charge. Free design advisory service if you send a plan of your garden to them.

Paints & Woodstains

Akzo Nobel Woodcare
Meadow Lane, St Ives, Cambridgeshire PE27 4UY
Stockists nationwide, telephone for information.
Tel: 01480 496868
Fax: 01480 496801
Email: woodcare@stives.deconorth.com
Web: www.sadolin.co.uk
Excellent range of Sadolin woodstains, preservatives and opaque wood paints.

Casa Paint Co.
PO Box 77, Thame, Oxon OX9 3FZ
Tel: 01296 483150
Fax: 01296 482241
Email: info@casa-paint.com
Web: www.casa-paint.com
Bright paints that can be supplied with an exterior mixer so they are suitable for use outside. Available in Homebase or by mail order. Export is possible.

Farrow and Ball Ltd (showroom)
249 Fulham Road, London SW3 6HY
Tel: 020 7351 0273
Fax: 020 7351 0221
Email: farrow-ball@farrow-ball.com
Web: www.farrow-ball.com
Stockists nationwide, telephone 01202 876141 for information.
Mail order and export.

Specialist Plants

Apple Court
Hordle Lane, Hordle, Lymington, Hampshire SO41 0HU
Tel: 01590 642130
Fax: 01590 644220
Email: applecourt@btinternet.com
Web: www.AppleCourt.com
Good selection of ornamental grasses, ferns, daylilies and hostas. Mail order or visit by appointment.

Architectural Plants
Cooks Farm, Nuthurst, Horsham, West Sussex RH13 6LH
Tel: 01403 891772
Fax: 01403 891056
Web: www.architectural plants.com
Email: horsham@architecturalplants.com
Specialists in a exotic-looking plants, many of which are hardy.

Bloms Bulbs Limited
Primrose Nurseries, Melchbourne, Bedford MK44 1ZZ
Tel: 01234 709099
Fax: 01243 709799
Email: chrisblom@blomsbulbs.com
Web: www.blomsbulbs.com
Bulbs, particularly tulips. Mail order, export to USA.

The Conservatory
Gomshall Gallery, Gomshall, Surrey GU5 9LB
Tel: 01483 203019
Fax: 01483 203282
Email: order@conservatoryplants.com
Web: www.conservatoryplants.com
Plants for conservatories, orangeries and swimming pools, including citrus trees, bougainvilleas, olives and more unusual plants.

David Austin Roses Ltd
Bowling Green Lane, Albrighton, Wolverhampton, West Midlands WV7 3HB
Tel: 01902 376300
Fax: 01902 372142
Email: retail@davidaustinroses.com
Roses, also peonies, iris and daylilies and a range of other hardy plants. Mail order, export or visit the nursery.

Fibrex Nurseries
Honeybourne Road, Pebworth, Stratford-on-Avon, Warwickshire CV37 8XT
Tel: 01789 720788
Fax: 01789 721162
Email: sales@fibrex.co.uk
Web: www.fibrex.co.uk
Specialists in ivies, ferns, pelargoniums and hellebores. Telephone for catalogue. Visit or mail order available.

J & D Marston
Culag, Green Lane, Nafferton, Driffield, East Yorkshire YO25 0LF
Tel/Fax: 01377 254487
Ferns and ornamental leadwork. Mail order and export available or visit by appointment.

Jacques Amand Ltd
The Nurseries, Clamp Hill, Stanmore, Middlesex HA7 3JS
Tel: 020 8420 7110
Fax: 020 8954 6784
Email: John.Amand@btinternet.com
Bulbs, including rare and unusual, from cultivated stock (not from the wild). Mail order, export worldwide or visit.

Jekka's Herb Farm
Rose Cottage, Shellard's Lane, Alveston, Bristol, Avon BS35 3SY
Tel: 01454 418878
Fax: 01454 411988
Email: farm@jekkasherb.demon.co.uk
Web: www.jekkasherbfarm.com
Herbs and wild flowers. Mail order, export.

Mallet Court Nursery
Curry Mallet, Taunton, Somerset TA3 6SY
Tel: 01823 480748
Fax: 01823 481009
Email: harris@malletcourt.freeserve.co.uk
Huge range of Japanese maples. Mail order or visit. Telephone for a catalogue.

The Palm Centre
Ham Central Nursery, Ham Street, Ham, Richmond, Surrey TW10 7HA
Tel: 0208 255 6191
Fax: 0208 255 6192
Email: mail@palmcentre.co.uk
Web: www.palmcentre.co.uk
Specialists in exotic palms.

Peter Beales Roses
London Road, Attleborough, Norfolk NR17 1AY
Tel: 01953 454700
Fax: 01953 456845
Email: sales@classicroses.co.uk
Web: www.classicroses.co.uk
Over 1,000 varieties of roses, old-fashioned varieties a speciality. Mail order, export or visit. Free catalogue.

P W Plants
Sunnyside, Heath Road, Kenninghall, Norfolk NR16 2DS
Tel/Fax: 01953 888212
Email: p.w.plants@paston.co.uk
Specialists in bamboo; also grasses and other foliage plants. Mail order and telephone ordering or visit the nursery.

Rickard's Hardy Ferns
Kyre Park, Kyre, Tenbury Wells, Worcestershire WR15 8RP
Tel: 01885 410282
Fax: 01885 410729
Specialists in ferns and tree ferns. Mail order or visit.

The Romantic Garden
Swannington, Norwich, Norfolk NR9 5NW
Tel: 01603 261488
Fax: 01603 864231
Email: enquiries@romantic-garden.demon.co.uk
Web: www.romantic-garden.demon.co.uk
Specialists in topiary and ornamental standards, also conservatory plants. Telephone for a catalogue; mail order.

Sculpture & Art

Allison Armour Associates
Baldhorns Park, Rusper, West Sussex RH12 4QU
Tel: 01293 871575
Fax: 01293 871111
Email: allisona@netcomuk.co.uk
Modern sculptures, including a glass ball with water running over its surface (AquaLens) and a mirror obelisk. Also, virtually invisible Perspex loungers.

Boldstone Sculpture
135 Boston Manor Road, Brentford, Middlesex TW8 9JR
Tel: 020 8568 9624
Tel/Fax: 020 8568 1658
Email: sally.v.price@binternet.com
Cast-stone wall sculptures (plaques), which can be hung or set into walls.

Foliole Fountain Project
6 Park Terrace, Tillington, Petworth, West Sussex GU28 9AE
Tel: 01798 344114
Contemporary metal fountain sculptures that look like plants.

The Hannah Pescar Sculpture Garden
Black and White Cottage, Standon Lane, Ockley, Surrey RH5 5QR
Tel: 01306 627269
Web: www.hannahpescarsculpture.com
Modern sculpture displayed in a garden. Open in summer and by appointment only in winter.

Christopher Marvell
The Old Rising Sun, Apthorpe Street, Fulbourn, Cambridge CB1 5EY
Tel/Fax: 01223 880444
Email: chris@marvell.abelgratis.net
Web: www.christophermarvell.co.uk
Contemporary garden sculpture. Visit the studio or telephone for images.

Corinne Stevens
Tel: 020 8376 2916
Email: muralmamma@hotmail.com
Murals

Water

Anthony Archer-Wills Ltd
Broadford Bridge Road, West Chiltington, West Sussex RH20 2LF
Tel: 01798 813204
Fax: 01798 815080
Water-garden design, construction, repairs and maintenance, consultation visits, pond planting schemes. Aquatic plant: visit the nursery or mail order.

Stapeley Water Gardens Ltd
London Road, Stapeley, Nantwich, Cheshire CW5 7LH
Tel: 01270 623868
Fax: 01270 624919
Email: stapeleywg@btinternet.com
Web: www.stapeleywatergardens.com
Europe's largest water-garden centre: fish, fountains, water and bog plants. National collection of water lilies. Mail order and informative and inexpensive catalogue available.

Water Techniques Ltd
Downside Mill, Cobham Park Road,
Cobham, Surrey KT11 3PF
Tel: 01932 866588
Fax: 01932 860200
Email: watteq@aol.com
*Design and supply of water features
from waterfalls to fountains.
Installation team recommended.*

Miscellaneous

The Crafts Council
44a Pentonville Road, London N1 9BY
Tel: 020 7278 7700
Fax: 020 7837 6891
Web: www.craftscouncil.org.uk
*National register of craftspeople,
including makers of furniture, mosaics,
wicker, stained glass and sculpture.*

Eatons Seashells
Tel/fax: 020 8539 5288
Email: EatonsSeashells@freenet.co.uk
*Large range, including craft shells and
mother of pearl inlay. Mail order only.*

The English Gardening School
Chelsea Physic Garden, 66 Royal
Hospital Road, London SW3 4HS
Tel: 020 7352 4347
Fax: 020 7376 3936
Email: egs@dircon.co.uk
Web: www.EnglishGardeningSchool.
co.uk
*Design, planting and horticulture
courses from one day to one year, either
at the school or by correspondence.*

LASSCO
Saint Michaels, Mark Street,
London EC2A 4ER
Tel: 020 7749 9944
Fax: 020 7749 9941
Email: st.michaels@lassco.co.uk
(original pieces), replicas@lassco.co.uk
(reproduction pieces)
Web: www.lassco.co.uk
*Architectural salvage, including garden
ornament, furniture and pots.
Reproduction furniture, gazebos,
columns, urns, sundials and fountains.
Export worldwide.*

Do-it-yourself

B&Q
2 Larch Drive, Gunnersbury
Avenue, Chiswick Roundabout,
London W4 5QL
Tel: 020 8995 8028
Web: www.diy.com
*Wide range of do-it-yourself products,
garden products and selection of
plants. Stores nationwide. Telephone
0800 444840 for details.*

Homebase
195 Warwick Road, London W14 8PU
Tel: 020 7603 6397
Web: www.homebase.co.uk
*Wide range of do-it-yourself and,
garden products. Selection of plants,
including seasonal, indoor and outdoor.
Telephone 0870 9008098 for stores
nationwide. Buy online at the Website.*

USA

Furniture

Adirondack Designs
350 Cypress Street
Fort Bragg, CA 95437
Tel: (800) 222 0343
Fax: (707) 964 2701
Web: www.adirondackdesign.com
*Adirondack furniture. Mail order
also available.*

Brown Jordan Co.
9860 Gidley Street, El Monte, CA 91731
Tel: (626) 443 8971
Web: www.brownjordancompany.com
*Metal furniture. Call for a catalog or a
stockist near you.*

Country Casual
17317 Germantown Road
Germantown, MD 20874
Tel: (301) 540 0040
Fax: (301) 540 7364
*High-quality teak furniture. Telephone
for catalog. Mail order available.*

Crate & Barrel
311 Gilman Avenue, PO Box 9059
Wheeling, IL 60090-9059
Tel: (800) 451 8217 or (847) 215 0025
Web: www.crateandbarrel.com
*Good value furniture, homewares and
accessories. Nationwide locations; call
for a catalog or store near you.*

Ethan Allen
Ethan Allen Drive, PO Box 1966
Danbury, CT 06813-1966
Tel: (800) 228 9229 or (203) 743 8304
Web: www.ethanallen.com
*Architecturally inspired indoor/outdoor
furniture in aluminium, from classic to
contemporary. Nationwide locations;
call for information.*

French Wyres
PO Box 131655, Tyler, TX 75713
Tel: (903) 561 1742
Web: frenchwyres.com
*Fine wire chairs, tables, plant stands
and window boxes. Mail order. Call
for a catalog.*

Gardener's Eden
1655 Bassford Drive
Mexico, MO 65265-1382
Tel: (800) 822 9600
Fax: 573 581 7361
*Furniture, accessories and tools. Nation-
wide locations. Mail order available.*

Home Depot
Web: www.HomeDepot.com
*Wide selection of outdoor furniture
and plants at discounted prices.*

Ikea
1100 Broadway Mall
Hicksville, NY 11801
Tel: (519) 681 4532
Web: www.ikea.com
*Scandinavian-style garden furniture
and accessories. Call (800) 434 IKEA for
a catalog or your local store. Mail order.*

Barbara Israel Garden Antiques
296 Mount Holly Road
Katonah, NY 1053
Tel: (212) 744 6281
Fax: (212) 744 2188
Web: www.bi-gardenantiques.com
*Period garden furniture from America
and imported from England, France
and Italy. Call or write with your
requirements, and photos of what is
available will be sent to you.*

Lowe's Home Improvement
Warehouse, PO Box 1111
North Wilkesboro, NC 28656
Tel: (336) 658 4000
Web: www.lowes.com
*Everything from lumber and power
tools to plants and outdoor furniture.*

Palecek, Inc
PO Box 225, Richmond, CA 94808
Tel: (800) 274 7730
Web: www.palecek.com
*Wicker, rattan and wooden furniture.
Call for a stockist near you.*

Pottery Barn
PO Box 379905, Las Vegas, NV 89137
Tel: (800) 588 6250
Web: www.potterybarn.com
*Furniture, homewares and accessories.
Nationwide locations. Call (800) 922
5507 for a catalog.*

Smith & Hawken
PO Box 431, Milwaukee WI 53201-0431
Tel: (800) 776 3336
Web: www.smithandhawken.com
*Furniture, accessories, tools and
plants. Nationwide locations. Mail
order available.*

The Wicker Works
267 Eighth Street
San Francisco, CA 94103
Tel: (415) 626 6730
*Elegant furniture in teak and wicker.
Stores nationwide; call for one near you.*

Willsboro Wood Products
S Ausable Street, PO Box 509
Keeseville NY 12944
Tel: (800) 342 3373
Furniture. Mail order available.

Paints & Woodstains

Akzo Nobel Woodcare
Stockists nationwide, telephone
for information.
Tel: 01480 496868
Fax: 01480 496801
Email: woodcare@stives.deconorth.com
Web: www.sadolin.co.uk
*Excellent range of Sadolin woodstains,
preservatives and opaque wood paints.*

Farrow and Ball (North America)
Stockists nationwide, telephone
for information.
Tel: (845) 3694912
Fax: (845) 3694913
Email: farrowball.na@mindspring.com
Web: www.farrow-ball.com
Mail order and export.

Farrow and Ball (Canada)
1054 Yonge Street, Toronto,
Ontario M4W 2LI
Tel: (877) 363 1040
Fax: (416) 920 1223
Email: fandb@istar.ca
Web: www.farrow-ball.com
Mail order and export.

Plants

Antique Rose Emporium
9300 Lueckemeyer Road
Brenham, TX 77833
Tel: (979) 836 9051
Web: www.weareroses.com
*Old roses, also perennials and ornamental
grasses. Mail order available.*

Blue Meadow Farm
184 Meadow Road
Montague, MA 01351
Tel: (413) 367 2394
Web: www.bluemeadowfarm.com
*Unusual perennial and annual plants.
Catalog but no mail order.*

Breck's US Reservation Center
3261 Garden View Lane
Walker, MI 49550-8000
Tel: (800) 722 9069
Fax: (800) 996 2852
Web: www.myseasons.com
All kinds of bulbs. Mail order, free catalog.

Canyon Creek Nursery
3527 Dry Creek Road
Oroville, CA 95965
Tel: (530) 533 2166
Web: www.canyoncreeknursery.com
Uncommon perennials.

Fox Hill Farm
434 W Michigan Avenue, PO Box 7
Parma, MI 49269
Tel: (517) 531 3179
All kinds of herbs. Mail order.

Gardens of the Blue Ridge
9056 Pittman Gap Road, Box 10
Pineola, NC 28662
Tel: (828) 733 2417
Wildflowers and ferns. Mail order.

Glasshouse Works
Church St, PO Box 97
Stewart, OH 45778-0097
Tel: (614) 662 2142
Web: www.glasshouseworks.com
*Houseplants, tropicals and exotics for
containers. Mail order.*

Greenlee Nursery
241 E Franklin Ave, Pomona, CA 91766
Tel: (909) 629 9045
Web: www.johngreenlee.com
*Ornamental grasses. Mail
order available.*

Jackson & Perkins
1310 Center Drive J
Medford, OR 97501
Tel: (541) 864 2388
Web: jacksonandperkins.com
*Wide selection of roses. Mail order.
phone for a catalog.*

Limerock Ornamental Grasses
70 Sawmill Road
Port Matilda, PA 16870
Tel: (814) 692 2272
Ornamental grasses. Mail order.

Logee's Greenhouses
141 North Street
Danielson CT 06239-1939
Tel: (888) 330 8038 or (860) 774 8038
Fax: (888) 774 9932
Web: www.logees.com
*Houseplants, tropicals and exotics
for containers. Mail order.*

Merry Gardens
Upper Mechanic St, Box 595
Camden, ME 04843
Tel: (207) 236 9064
*Ivies, pelargoniums and herbs.
Mail order.*

Old House Gardens
536 W Third Street
Ann Arbor, MI 48103-4957
Tel: (734) 995 1486
Fax: (734) 995 1687
Email: OHGBulbs@aol.com
*Antique-type flower bulbs and tubers.
Mail order only.*

Park Seed Company, Inc.
1 Parkton Avenue
Greenwood, SC 29647-0001
Tel: (800) 845 3369
Fax: (800) 275 9941
Web: www.parkseed.com
Extensive seed collection. Mail order.

Shady Oaks Nursery
400 15th Avenue SE, Waseca, MN 56093
Tel: (507) 835 5033
Web: www.shadyoaks.com
*Specialists in plants for shady areas.
Mail order.*

Tools & Accessories

Anthropologie
235 S 17th Street
Philadelphia, PA 19103
Tel: (215) 564 2313
Web: www.anthropologie.com
*Selection of accessories and flowerpots.
Nationwide locations; call for a store
near you.*

Capital Garden Products
Schieren Associates Ltd, PO Box 400
Pottersville, NJ 07979
Tel: (908) 439 2120
Fax: (908) 439 2113
*High quality, attractive fibreglass
containers and wall fountains.
Also aluminium, steel and canvas
garden furniture. Mail order and
export worldwide.*

Colonial Williamsburg
PO Box 3532, Williamsburg, VA 23185
Tel: (800) 446 9240
Web: www.williamsburgmarketplace.
com
*Hurricane lamps, candlestick and other
garden accessories. Mail order
available. Catalog.*

Gardener's Supply Co.
128 Intervale Road
Burlington, VT 05401
Tel: (800) 863 1700 or (800) 955 3370
Web: www.gardeners.com
Tools and accessories. Mail order.

Kinsman Co.
PO Box 428, 6805 Easton Road
Pipersville PA 18947
Tel: (800) 733 4146 or (215) 766 5604
Fax: (215) 766 5624
Web: www.kinsmangarden.com
*Tools and accessories. Mail
order available.*

Kenneth Lynch & Sons
84 Danbury Road, Wilton CT 06897
Tel: (203) 762 8363
Web: www.klynchandsons.com
*Garden Ornaments. Mail
order available.*

Urban Farmer Store
2833 Vincente Street
San Francisco, CA 94116
Tel: (800) 753 3745 or (416) 661 2204
Web: www.urbanfarmerstore.com
Tools and accessories. Mail order.

Water

Lilypons Water Gardens
7000 Lilypons Rd, PO Box 10
Buckeystown, MD 21717
Tel: (800) 723 7667
*Water plants, fish and aquatic supplies.
Mail order available.*

Paradise Water Gardens
14 May Street, Whitman MA 02382
Tel: (781) 447 4711
Web: www.paradisewatergardens.com
Mail order.

Van Ness Water Gardens
2460 North Euclid Avenue
Upland CA 91784-1199
Tel: (909) 982 2425
Fax: (909) 949 7217
Web: www.vannesswatergardens.com
Mail order.

Wood & Stone

Bamboo Fencer
179 Boylston Street
Jamaica Plain, MA 02130
Tel: (617) 524 6137
Web: www.bamboofencer.com
*Fencing, gates and pergolas made
of bamboo. Across the country and
worldwide. Mail order. Call for a catalog.*

Bear Creek Lumber Co.
495 Twisp Winthrop Road, PO Box 669
Winthrop WA 98862
Tel: (800) 597 7191
Fax: (509) 997 2040
Web: www.bearcreeklumber.com

High Plains Stone Co.
8585 N Us Highway 85
Littleton, CO 80125
Tel: (303) 791 1862
Web: www.highplainsstone.com

INDEX

Figures in *italics* indicate captions.

abutilon, trailing 149
Abutilon megapotamicum 149
acacia: golden false 147;
  mop-head 151
Acacia dealbata 92
Acanthus mollis 147
Acanthus spinosus 147
Acer japonicum 'Aconitifolium' 28
Acer palmatum 28, 103, 144, 147
Achillea 146; 'Coronation Gold'
  140, 146
aconites, winter 79
Aconitum 146
Adam's needle 35
Aeonium arboreum 'Atropurpureum' 70
aeoniums 70
Agave americana 35, 70, *102, 103, 105*
Ajuga 22
Ajuga reptans 150
Akebia quinata 86
Alchemilla mollis 45, 146, 147, 150
algae 128
Allium cristophii 49
Allium schoenoprasum 152–3
Allium schubertii 49
aloe vera 73
aloes 70
aluminium 77
Amelanchier lamarckii 145
ammonites 114
Anemone x hybrida 91, 149
anemones, Japanese 91, 149
arbours 58, 120
Arbutus unedo 61, 145, 151
arches 13, 19, 45, 119–20
Argyranthemum 104
Argyranthemum gracile
  'Chelsea Girl' 64
armchairs 82, 121
Artemisia sp. 42, 64
Artemisia alba 'Canescens' 140
artemisias 64
Arum italicum 79
Asarum 78
Asarum europaeum 85
aspect 10, 17
Astelia chathamica 'Silver Spear' 35
astilbes 147
astroturf 22, 33, 82, 112–13
awnings 12, 23, 52, 120
azaleas 37
Azolia filiculoides 126

back gardens and courtyards 18–55
balconies 10, 17, 61–2, 75, 97, 121
bamboo *10, 14, 37, 51, 61, 66, 69,*
  105, 113, 114, 143; black 143;
  black-stemmed 49; dwarf 79;
  dwarf evergreen 103; dwarf
  variegated 97; evergreen pygmy
  102; golden 143; pygmy 103;
  screening 117; spouts 37
bananas 24; Japanese hardy 142
barbecues 12, 23, 132
barberry 151; purple barberry 61, 144;
  purple dwarf 98
basements 7, 10, 14, 76–95
basil 102, 153
baskets, trug 45
bay 91, 98, 139, 153; sweet 42
beach hut *14*

beams 13, *20, 30,* 119, 120
bear's breeches 147
bedding plants 45, 95, 104, 149
beds 55
beech 117, 144
Begonia semperflorens 73, 91
begonias 70, 91, 95
bellflowers *19,* 61, 86; Chilean 142
  Dalmatian 61
Bellis perennis Pomponette Series 105
benches 12, 45, *51,* 62, 120, 121, 122
Berberis thunbergii 151; 'Atropurpurea
  Nana' 98; f. *atropurpurea* 144
Berberis x ottawensis 'Superba' 61
Bergenia 85, 150
Betula albosinensis var.
  septentrionalis 145
Betula pendula 61
Betula utilis 61
Betula utilis var. *jacquemontii* 28, 28
bidens 105, 140
biennials 145
birch: Chinese 145; Himalayan 61;
  silver 28, *28,* 61
birdbaths 131
bishop's mitre 150
blankets 12, 89, 113
bleeding heart 79
blue fescue *102, 103,* 152; small 103
blue plants 64
bluebells 79
bolsters 51
bonsai 37
borders *12,* 13
bougainvilleas 91
boundaries 97, 114–18
Bowles' golden sedge 103, 130, 147
box 30, 37, 85, 95, *98,* 102, 117,
  139, 144, 151
  green dwarf 98
boxes 23, 33, 59, 111, 137, 139
Brachycome 105
brick 22, 97, 104, 119; bricks
  109–10, 116
glass 14, 33, 117
broom 146, 151
buckets 55, 137, 140
buckthorn, Italian 98
bugle 22, 105, 150
buildings 135
bulbs: easy 148; planting 148
bullrushes 30
busy lizzies 70, 91, 95, 105
Buxus sempervirens 98, 98, 144

cabbage 30; ornamental 105;
  skunk 139
cabbage palm 35, 70, 98
Calamagrostis x acutiflora 'Karl
  Foerster' 152
*Calamondin x citrofortunella
  microcarpa 91,* 92
Calendula officinalis 105
camellias 10, 37, 78, 91, 151
Campanula portenschlagiana 19, 61
candles 12, 13, 23, 24, 45, 51, 55, 80,
  80, 89, 124, 125
canopy *80*
cape figwort 146
Carex comans bronze 152
Carex elata 'Aurea' 130
Carex hachijoensis 'Evergold' 103, 152
Carex pendula 130
carpets 52
Carpinus betulus 144
carrots 30

castor oil plant 78, *78,* 85, 104,
  142–3, 151
Catalpa bignonioides 'Aurea' 151
catmint (catnip) 42, 45, 61, 150
Ceanothus 151
Centranthus ruber 146
century plant 35, 70, *102, 103, 105*
Ceratostigma willmottianum 145
Chaenomeles 37, 151
Chaenomeles speciosa 145
chain-link fences 116
chairs 12, *19,* 22, *41,* 45, 51, 55, 62, *62,*
  82, 91, 123, 135
chandeliers 89, *89,* 124
checkerberry 105
cherry 66; flowering 37; great white
  151; Japanese 151; Japanese
  flowering 27; Tibetan 145; wild 151
ch'i 69
chimneypots 59, 140
china 55, 89
Chinese Oriental style 66, 69, *69*
chives 152–3
Chlorophytum comosum
  'Variegatum' *92*
chocolate plant 42
Choisya ternata 78, 85, 151
Christmas box 79, 99, 151
Cistus 91
Cistus x purpureus 146, 151
Citrus limon 92
citrus trees 52, 91, 139
classical style 95
clematis 45, 86, 119
Clematis alpina 142
Clematis armandii 92, 99, 119
Clematis macropetala 142
Clematis montana 141
Clematis montana var. *rubens*
  'Elizabeth' 119
climbers *19,* 20, 22, 45, 57, 58, 77, 91,
  95, 97, 115, 116, 119, 142, 151
cloches 133
club rush 130
cobblestones 22, 37, 62, 75, *75,* 91, 97,
  98, 110, 127
cold frame 13
columns 95
compost 27, 59, 105; aquatic 126;
  ericaceous 91
concrete 14, 22, 30, 33, 49, 51, 75, *75,*
  78, 97, 109, 116, 137, 139
container planting 105
containers 10, 13, 17, 33, 49, 52, 55, 58–9,
  62, 75, 78, 91, 99, 101, 102, 137–40;
decorating 101–2
irrigation for 136
Convallaria 79
Convolvulus cneorum 64
copper 119, 140
coral flower 143–4
Cordyline australis 35, 70, *98*
coriander 153
Coriandrum sativum 153
Corokia cotoneaster 49
corten 113
Cornus alba 151; 'Elegantissima' 145
Cornus alternifolia 'Argentea' 28
courtyards 23; Moroccan 51, *51,* 52, *52*
crab apples 145, 151
cranesbill 146, 150; Balkan 146, 150;
  meadow 153

Crassula ovata 70
Crataegus laevigata 'Paul's Scarlet' 61
Crataegus monogyna 61
Cratoegus 61
Crocosmia 24, 61
crocuses 108, 148, 153
cubes 33, 51
cupboards 23
curtains 77, 117, 119
cushions 12, *14,* 24, 27, 37, 45, 51,
  52, 59, *69, 80, 82,* 89, 91, 113,
  121, 122, 135
cuttings 13
cyclamen 79, 105
Cyclamen hederifolium 105
Cyperus involucratus 130
Cytisus 146, 151

daffodils 148; dwarf 108
dahlias 70
daisies: *Bellis* 105; blue 149;
  Livingstone 105; ox-eye 153;
  Swan River 105
daphne 79, 151
Daphne bholua 151
Daphne odora 99, 151
Daphne x burkwoodii 151
Darmera peltata 130
daybeds 51
dead nettles 150; golden spotted 147
deadheading 46
decking 7, *12,* 22, 33, 55, 58, *62,* 73, 78,
  111, 117, 122
diascias 105
Dicentra 79
Dicksonia antarctica 143
dogwood 151; pagoda 28;
  variegated 145
doors 20, 34, 97, 98, 99
dragons, carved 66
drainage 58–9, 91, 138, 148, 152
dressing up your garden 41, *41,* 42, *42*
driftwood 37, 75
drinks bar 73
Dryopteris filix-mas 104

Echeveria 98
echeverias 70
edible flowers 146
Eichhornia crassipes 126
Elaeagnus x ebbingei 61, 151
elder 151; blackish-purple 75;
  common 61; golden 147
elephant's ears 85, 150
entertaining 9, 12
Epimedium x perralchicum 150
Equisetum 130
Erica carnea 105
Erigeron karvinskianus 149
Eriobotrya japonica 147
Eryngium 34, 35, 64
Erysimum 'Bowles Mauve' 149
Eschscholzia 147
Eucalyptus pauciflora subsp.
  niphophila 28
Euonymus fortunei 104, 105, 151
Euonymus japonicus 'Ovatus aureus' *98*
Euonymus 'Silver Queen' 85
Euphorbia amygdaloides var. *robbiae*
  85, 104, 150
Euphorbia characias 91
Euphorbia characias subsp. *wulfenii* 64
Euphorbia myrsinites 102
evening primrose 42
evergreens 13, 20, 20, 78, 98, 99, *101,*
  103; shade-tolerant 85

ACKNOWLEDGEMENTS

I would like to acknowledge the kind cooperation of the garden owners and garden designers who gave permission to photograph their beautiful gardens: 96 The Academy; 12 Rob Brewster (designer); 11, 50, 51, 52, 53 Bo Chapman; 99 (top), 118 (left) Mr and Mrs Deacon; 21, 28–9, 30, 32–3, 34, 127, 132, 134 (below), 135 (below) Penny Duke; 116 James Fraser (trellis); 62, 63, 74 Catherine Gratwicke; 15, 20, 25, 26, 27, 99 (below), 105, 115, 123 (right), 128, 135 (top), 153 Robin Green and Ralph Cade; 84, 102, 103, 110 (below), 136 (top) Alison Jenkins (designer); 143 (right), 151 Tim Leunig and Julia Cerrutti; 76, 90, 93 Zia Mattocks; 16, 18, 40, 79, 109, 136 (below) Keith and Maureen McKee; 6, 43, 44, 45, 56, 110 (top) Helen Ong, Townscapes Landscape Contractors (garden builder); 13, 120 (below) Ross Palmer (designer); 54, 55, 87, 88 Russell and Fiona Porter; 8, 59, 66, 67, 68, 69 Hilary Robertson; 118 (right), 126, 138 Jo Scott; 4–5, 94 Corinne Stevens (mural painter); 36, 38, 39, 98, 119, 131 John Tordoff (designer); 48, 49, 120 (left), 122 (right), 124, 125 (below), 129 Charles Worthington, Stephen Woodhams (designer).

Robin Green and Ralph Cade, and John Tordoff open their London gardens under the National Gardens Scheme – details of the openings can be found in *Gardens of England and Wales Open For Charity* ('the yellow book'), under Greater London.

Many thanks to Prêt-à-pot, who lent their gorgeous glazed and galvanized pots, and Patio Garden Centre, who lent many lovely pots and plants.

I would like to give a big hug to my mother, Susie Heybrook, for inspiring me and giving me the gardening bug. I would also like to thank Sarah Bravo for suggesting I start writing about gardening, Cath Gratwicke for her beautiful photographs and, last but not least, the team at Carlton Books, in particular Zia Mattocks and Barbara Zuñiga, for the great job they have done.